Arthur Milnor Bridgman

A Souvenir of Massachusetts Legislators

Arthur Milnor Bridgman

A Souvenir of Massachusetts Legislators

ISBN/EAN: 9783744730921

Printed in Europe, USA, Canada, Australia, Japan

Cover: Foto ©ninafisch / pixelio.de

More available books at **www.hansebooks.com**

Massachusetts Legislators,

1898.

VOLUME VII

Issued Yearly By

A. M. BRIDGMAN,
STOUGHTON, MASS.

Copyrighted 1897 by

A. M. BRIDGMAN.

Half-tone and Text Print by Stoughton Record Print, Stoughton
Half-tones from Photos. from Elmer Chickering, the "Royal Photographer," 21 West Street, Boston
Half-tones, Aznive Engraving Co., 375 Washington Street, Boston.

PREFACE.

The Editor of the Souvenir has had occasion to remark in previous editions that each Legislature has some peculiar characteristic to distinguish it from all others. It fell to the lot of the Legislature of 1898, for the first time in over 30 years, or the usual span of a generation, to make war preparations and to discuss war measures. The breaking out of the war with Spain found our Legislature ready to do its part promptly and patriotically. With absolute unanimity and no more delay than was necessary for the making of the proper motions and the signature of the bill by Governor Wolcott, the whole transaction occupying less than half an hour, the war appropriation of half a million dollars was voted; and in the Senate the enactment of the measure was greeted with three cheers. No partisan discussion but patriotic action marked every measure of similar import. But this Souvenir is not intended as a record of what was done. It is only a "Souvenir" of those who did,—their pictures, their biographical sketches, and their autographs, so that generations to come may know who they were and how they looked; and also to show the halls wherein they performed so well their parts. What they did is recorded elsewhere; here are the men of whom these acts are recorded. Each year brings new features of improvement to the Souvenir, as well as to all other progressive things. The new views in this Souvenir add not a little to its permanent value. The Legislature of 1898 had much important public work to do; and that which it had to do it did well. Like all other Legislatures it had its critics, and yet it doubtless well represented the prevailing thought and sentiment of the state.

A. M. BRIDGMAN, Editor.

THE STATE HOUSE.

Showing Beacon Street in Front, Through Which Have Marched the Troops to be Reviewed by the Governor.

His Excellency ROGER WOLCOTT, Governor.

THE GOVERNOR'S PRIVATE ROOM.

Upon the wall (left) Painting of Gov. Gaston, (center) Gov. Long now U. S. Secy. of Navy, (right) Gov. Rice; bust of Gov. Greenhalge in center.

Hon. W. M. OLIN, Secretary. Hon. E. P. Shaw, Treasurer.
His Honor WINTHROP MURRAY CRANE, Lieutenant Governor.
Hon. J. W. KIMBALL, Auditor. Hon. H. M. KNOWLTON, Atty-General.

ROOM OF EXECUTIVE COUNCIL.

In Sessions of the Council the Governor sits in the larger chair in the center, and the Lieutenant Governor at his right.

THE EXECUTIVE COUNCIL.

Hon. N. T. Ryder.   Hon. B. S. Lovell.   Hon. G. N. Swallow.
Hon. J. H. Sullivan.   Hon. H. H. Atherton.
Hon. E. H. Shaw.   Hon. A. L. Joslin.   Hon. W. B. Plunkett.
James M. Perkins.   Edward F. Hamlin.

SENATE CHAMBER.
From the rear, facing the desk of the President, and the Reporters' Gallery, the National and State Flags and Coat-of-arms.

SENATE CHAMBER.
From southwest corner, showing Ladies' Gallery opposite.

ROOM OF PRESIDENT OF THE SENATE.

OFFICERS OF THE SENATE.

H. D. COOLIDGE, Clerk.   REV. EDMUND DOWSE, Chaplain.
Hon. GEORGE E. SMITH, President.
W. H. SANGER, Assistant Clerk.   K. T. TAYLOR, Clerical Assistant.

RECEPTION ROOM OF THE SENATE.
Formerly the Senate Chamber in the old "Bulfinch" State House. The paintings on the walls are of former Governors, mainly those of colonial times.

THE SENATE READING ROOM.

ROOM OF THE SPEAKER OF THE HOUSE

OFFICERS OF THE HOUSE.
Hon. John L. Bates, Speaker.
J. W. Kimball, Clerk.   Rev. D. W. Waldron, Chaplain
F. E. Bridgman, Assistant Clerk.

DORIC HALL.

This hall has seen varied gatherings, but none of greater interest than that of April 17, 1861. On that day, the first volunteer company of the whole country, during the late War of the Rebellion, assembled here, chose its officers, received overcoats from the government and in an hour and a half from the time of assembling was on its way to the front. The story, in more detail, is as follows: In Cambridge, in 1860, had been formed a company of "Wide Awakes" to help elect President Lincoln. Hon. J. M. S. Williams, congressman from that district, promised them that if they would keep up their organization they could go to Washington to see Lincoln inaugurated. But the United State government forbade the assembling of such bodies at the national capital. During the dark days of February, 1861, several of the company agreed to volunteer if they were needed, and, on the 14th of February, several of them signed an agreement to that effect. First on the list was the name of John Kinnear, now assistant doorkeeper of the House. In the first week in March, he, with a few others, visited the State House and personally tendered their services to Governor Andrew. He advised them that there was no immediate need of their services and that they return to Cambridge, whence he would summon them if necessary. Then came the news of the breaking out of rebellion. They at once visited the State House, finding Governor and Council in session. Governor Andrew told them to return to Cambridge and that they would receive orders in an hour. They returned and the orders speedily reached them. Then, again, they hastened to the State House, many of their members leaving their work and throwing their tools into the street. Reaching the State House, they assembled in Doric Hall, ninety-seven of them. In a small adjoining room they chose officers, electing James Prentice Richardson, now of Texas, as captain. They first went to the Old Colony station, but were soon ordered to the "S. R. Spaulding", where they embarked for Fortress Monroe. They were first assigned to the Fifth regiment, but were soon transferred to the Third, becoming Company C. This was, without doubt, the first volunteer company of the late war. It is a matter of history that this prompt, loyal and general response of this company, in contrast with the scattering returns from more pretentious organizations, did much to encourage the State authorities and "the great war Governor."

In this hall lay, in state, the body of Charles Sumner, Sunday, March 15, 1874, where it was viewed by a multitude as vast as time would allow.

In this hall gathered the "Army of the Unemployed", February 20, 1894, whence they were removed by detachments of the district and Boston police, but without violence. They had just been addressed on the Capitol steps by Governor Greenhalge.

This view is taken from the main entrance and shows the statues of Washington and John A. Andrew in the distance.

DORIC HALL.

THE STATE LIBRARY.

Upon the Safe in the Foreground, under a glass case, rests the famous Manuscript History of "Plimouth Plantation" by Gov. Wm. Bradford, 1621.

COMMITTEE ON AGRICULTURE.

Hon. G. E. Putnam.   Hon. C. O. Bailey.   T. W. Crocker.   A. F. Adams.
F. P. Bennett, House Chairman.   G. E. Bemis, Clerk.
            Hon. H. R. Barber, Chairman.
C. E. Parker.   A. D. King.   A. F. Hiscox.   Horatio Bisbee.

COMMITTEE ON BANKS AND BANKING.

Hon. H. Parsons.   Hon. R. A. Soule.   C. F. Sullivan.   O. M. Gove.
Wm Curtis, House Chairman.   C. F. How, Clerk.
              Hon. W. A. Whittlesey, Chairman.
Amos E. Hall.   L. G. McKnight.   C. D. Lewis.   H. L. Stalker.

COMMITTEE ON CITIES.

Hon. A. S. Roe   Hon. C. F. Folsom.   J. F. Sheehan.
                          Hon. L. E. Chamberlain.
W. H. I. Hayes, House Chairman.   Saml. Cole, Clerk.
              Hon G. E. Putnam, Chairman.
F. W. Estey.   M. D. Gilman.   Fred Hammond.   A. T. Folsom.
P. F. Tague.   G. F. Harwood.   A. H. Burgess.   D. J. Kane.

COMMITTEE ON CONSTITUTIONAL AMENDMENTS.
Hon. F. W. Dallinger.   Hon. W. R. Black.   A. R. Crosby.   J. W. Grimes.
A. W. Lyon, House Chairman.   C. R. Saunders, Clerk.
Hon. R. W. Irwin, Chairman.
W. A. Nettleton.   W. I. McLoughlin.   W. E. Mahoney   G. S. Selfridge.

COMMITTEE ON COUNTIES.

Hon. F. W. Dallinger.   Hon. J. J. Flynn.   M. D. Jones.   W. H. Marden.
H. H. Bosworth, House Chairman.   L. J. Macken, Clerk.
                Hon. W. W. Leach, Chairman.
M. B. Jones.   F. H. Farmer.   H. J. Draper.   E. E. Wentworth.

COMMITTEE ON DRAINAGE.

HON. E. W. ROBERTS.   HON. H. PARSONS.   G. B. SMART.   R. M. ALLEN.
J. A. POWERS, House Chairman.   W. H. SEVERANCE, Clerk.
                HON. J. C. BENNETT, Chairman.
J. BOTTOMLY.   E. J. TWOMEY.   GEO. BALCOM.   F. W. BARNARD.

COMMITTEE ON EDUCATION.

Hon. J. H. Flint. Hon. J. J. Flynn. Francis Leland. A. P. Williams.
B. Porter, Jr., House Chairman. W. L. Morse, Clerk.
Hon. A. S. Roe, Chairman.
F. F. Phillips. G. H. Norton. J. W. Hill. W. A. Nettleton.

COMMITTEE ON ELECTIONS.

J. B. L. BARTLETT, Chairman. LUTHER HALL. A. R. CROSBY.
J. B. DUMOND. N. G. STAPLES. H. V. CROSBY. D. A. MAHONEY.

COMMITTEE ON PAY ROLL.

G. H. BARTLETT, Chairman. WARREN BOYNTON. THOMAS MACKEY.

COMMITTEE ON ELECTION LAWS.

Hon. S. W. George.   Hon. C. L. Quirk.   F. P. Bennett.   T. J. Dooling.
O. C. Blaney, House Chairman.   A. E. Wells, Clerk.
            Hon. W. W. Davis, Chairman.
T. M. Denham.   E. E. Donovan.   C. R. Saunders.   H. W. Bresnahan.

COMMITTEE ON ENGROSSED BILLS (Senate.)
Hon. W. P. Fairbank, Chairman.   Hon. C. O. Bailey.   Hon. C. I. Quirk.
COMMITTEE ON BILLS IN THIRD READING (Senate.)
Hon. L. E. Chamberlain, Chairman. Hon. J. B. Farley. Hon. J. D H. Gauss.
COMMITTEE ON ENGROSSED BILLS (House.)
A. S. Wood, Chairman.   Saml. Cole.   J. H. Joubert.
COMMITTEE ON BILLS IN THIRD READING (House.)
F. E. Crawford, Chairman.   A. S. Apsey.   M. L. Breath.

COMMITTEE ON FEDERAL RELATIONS.

Hon. W. H. Fairbank. Hon. D. D. Rourke. F. F. Farrar. J. O. Slocum.
E. B. Estes, House Chairman. W. S. Swift. Clerk.
Hon. H. Parsons. Chairman.
J. M. Philbrick. F. P. Drake. Wm. Bridgeo. T. A. Conroy.

COMMITTEE ON FISHERIES AND GAME.

Hon. W. A. Morse.   Hon. W. W. Davis.   W. A. Lang.   J. O. Slocum.
C. P. Mills, House Chairman.   H. C. Smith, Clerk.
            Hon. C. O. Bailey, Chairman.
J. M. Stevenson.   D. J. Gleason.   A. B. Fay.   T. D. Sears.

(43)

COMMITTEE ON HARBORS AND PUBLIC LANDS.

Hon. W. A. Morse.   Hon. J. C. Bennett.   C. E. Hoag.   J. A. McManus.
F. W. Francis, House Chairman.   L. W. Ross, Clerk.
             Hon. W. H. Hodgkins, Chairman.
A. W. Lyon.   Luther Hall.   Butler Ames.   A. M. Morrison.

COMMITTEE ON INSURANCE.

Hon. L. E. Chamberlain.   Hon. Wm. Moran.   R. F. Andrews, Jr.
H. L. Boutwell.
C. E. Brown, House Chairman.   F. C. Perry, Clerk.
Hon. J. H. Flint, Chairman.
T. C. Bachelder.   S. A. Allen.   D. J. Kiley.   J. F. Dalton.

COMMITTEE ON THE JUDICIARY.

HON. R. W. IRWIN.   HON. J. H. FLINT.   HON. C. I. QUIRK.
HON. F. H. WILLIAMS.
J. J. MYERS, House Chairman   C. H. INNES, Clerk.
HON. W. A. MORSE, Chairman.   W. B. STONE.
H. A. DUBUQUE.   H. C. ATTWILL.   J. E. MAGENIS.   L. W. PETERS.
H. H. NEWTON.   T. F. NOONAN.   E. J. WHITAKER.   W. J. MILLER.

COMMITTEE ON LABOR

Hon. Wm. Moran. Hon. W. W. Towle. F. E. Crawford. F. W. Barnard.
S. Ross, House Chairman.   T. Donahue, Clerk.
Hon. W. W. Leach, Chairman.
J. Whitehead.   R. Cullinane.   R. W. Garrity.   D. J. Driscoll.

COMMITTEE ON LIBRARIES.

Hon D. B. Shaw.   Hon. A. L. Harwood.   Saml. Ross.   N. G. Staples.
G. W. Coombs, House Chairman.   J. E. Baldwin, Clerk.
            Hon. W. W. Davis, Chairman.
J. H. Joubert.   H. V. Crosby.   M. E. Gaddis.   A. P. Learoyd.

COMMITTEE ON LIQUOR LAW.

Hon. D. B. Shaw.　　Hon. H. R. Barber.　　Almon F. Hall.　　John Bleiler.
T. H. Newcomb, House Chairman.　　　　　　　　　　E. B. Estes, Clerk.
Hon. W. H. Cook, Chairman.
J. J. Feneno.　　A. E. Hemphill.　　J. B. Dumond.　　J. A. Rowan.

COMMITTEE ON MANUFACTURES.

Hon. C. E. Folsom.   Hon. D. D. Rourke.   E. T. Rowell.   F. E. Huntress.
H. L. Boutwell, House Chairman.   G. G. Frederick, Clerk.
              Hon. C. F. Woodward, Chairman.
W. E. Skillings.   M. E. Hawes.   S. A. Tuttle.   O. S. Grant.

COMMITTEE ON MERCANTILE AFFAIRS.

Hon. W. W. Davis   Hon. J. A. Gallivan.   F. O. Winslow.   A. E. Hemphill.
H. A. Belcher, House Chairman.   J. L. Kelly, Clerk.
                    Hon. F. H. Williams, Chairman.
Wm. S. Kyle.   J. W. Connelly.   E. E. Willard.   D. W. Battles.

COMMITTEE ON METROPOLITAN AFFAIRS.

Hon. W. W. Towle.　　　Hon. C. F. Woodward.　　　E. L. Pickard.
　　　　　　　　　　　　　　　　Hon. D. D. Rourke.
G. R. Jones, House Chairman.　　　　　　　G. F. Mead, Clerk.
　　　　　　Hon. F. W. Dallinger, Chairman.
H. C. White.　　　J. I Stewart　　　S. F. Bickford.　　　C. O. Beede
C. P. Keith.　　　A. S. Hayes.　　　W. J. Miller.　　　C. S. Clerke.

COMMITTEE ON MILITARY AFFAIRS.

Hon. C. F. Woodward. Hon. W. L. Bouve. B. W. Mayo. L. G. McKnight.
W. H. Marden, House Chairman.   F. S. Richardson, Clerk.
Hon. W. H. Brigham, Chairman.
A. Campbell.   F. P. Harlow.   G. M. Rice.   Butler Ames.

COMMITTEE ON PARISHES AND RELIGIOUS SOCIETIES.
Hon. J. D. H. Gauss. Hon. W. B. Mahoney. C. P. Mills. G. L. Wihtcomb.
D. W. Davis, House Chairman.   F. O. Winslow, Clerk.
           Hon. E. B. Crane, Chairman.
W. S. Swift.   C. H. Ramsdell.   J. W. Hill.   Rufus Howe.

COMMITTEE ON PRINTING.

Hon. G. E. Putnam.   Hon. D. D. Rourke.   J. J. Gartland, Jr.
David G. Pratt.
G. F. Fuller, House Chairman.   D. W. Davis, Clerk.
Hon. W. R. Black, Chairman.
A. E. Wells.   Thomas Mackey   Warren Boynton.   H. C. Smith.

COMMITTEE ON PRISONS

Hon. H. R. Barber.   Hon. W. B. Mahoney.   C. W. Tilton.   J. E. Pattee.
T. M. Denham, House Chairman.   A. S. Wood, Clerk.
Hon. W. H. Cook, Chairman.
A. R. Snow   Thomas Donahue.   W. N. Newcomb.   J. E. Baldwin.

COMMITTEE ON PROBATE AND INSOLVENCY.

Hon. W. L. Bouve.   Hon. W. W. Leach.   C. R. Johnson.   John F Libby.
W. D. Chapple, House Chairman.   T. C. Bachelder, Clerk.
          Hon. W. W. Towle, Chairman.
Albert S. Apsey.   F. E. Huntress.   W. I. McLoughlin.   R. V. King.

COMMITTEE ON PUBLIC CHARITABLE INSTITUTIONS.
Hon W. H. Fairbank. Hon. Wm. Moran. E. C. Waterman. J. M. Stevenson.
J. J. Whipple, House Chairman- R S. Sisson, Clerk.
Hon. J. D. H. Gauss, Chairman.
L. B. Chandler. M. L Russell. D. S. Coolidge. C. S. Crouch

COMMITTEE ON PUBLIC HEALTH.

Hon. W. L. Bouve.   Hon. W. B. Mahoney.   G. B. Smart.   J. J. Whipple.
E. B. Callender, House Chairman.   W. J. Bullock, Clerk.
Hon. C. E. Folsom, Chairman.
W. Kells, Jr.   D. A. Mahoney.   F. H. Whitcomb.   E. C. Waterman.

COMMITTEE ON PUBLIC SERVICE.

Hon. J. B Farley. Hon G. E. Putnam. J. P. Ramsdell. G. W. Coombs.
F. F. Phillips, House Chairman.   J. P. Ramsay, Clerk.
Hon. S. W. George, Chairman.
T. W. Crocker.   M. L. Breath.   M. E. Gaddis.   J. F. Carberry.

COMMITTEE ON RAILROADS.

Hon. A. L. Harwood. Hon. J. B. Holden. Hon. W. H. Brigham. G. F. Fuller.
J. J. McCarthy. House Chairman.   S. D Reed, Clerk.
                    Hon. R. A. Soule, Chairman.
J. H. Ponce.   E. B. Nevin.   O. M. Gove.   C. E. Trow.
H. L. Stalker.   L. M. Haskins.   Albert Poor   Daniel England.

COMMITTEE ON ROADS AND BRIDGES.

Hon. W. R. Black.   Hon. E. B Crane.   W. A. Lang.   H. E. Gaylord.
J. W. Grimes, House Chairman.   R. E. Allen, Clerk.
            Hon. J. C. Bennett, Chairman.
B. W. Mayo.   H. C. Foster.   B. F. Stanley.   J. O'Connor.

COMMITTEE ON RULES.

Hon. J. B. Holden.   Hon. W. H. Brigham.   Hon. J. A. Gallivan.
Hon. F. H. Williams.
Speaker J. L. Bates, House Chairman.   J. J. Myers.
President G. E. Smith, Chairman.
G. R. Jones.   F. C. Lowell.   Albert Clarke.   W. B. Stone.
W. H. I. Hayes.   T. W. Kenefick.   H. C. Parsons.   J. J. McCarthy.

COMMITTEE ON STATE HOUSE.

Hon. A. S. Roe.   Hon. R. A. Soule.   M. D. Jones.   F. C. Perry.
G. W. Whidden, House Chairman.   W. E. Skillings, Clerk.
Hon. J. B. Holden, Chairman.
J. P. Ramsay.   R. Cullinane.   W. Kells, Jr.   A. P. Learoyd.

(85)

COMMITTEE ON STREET RAILWAYS.

Hon. E. B. Crane.   Hon. W. H. Hodgkins.   W. S. V. Cooke.
Hon. C. O. Bailey.
E. H. Hoyt, House Chairman.   J. C. Anthony, Clerk.
Hon. R. I. Irwin, Chairman.
E. B. Callender.   W. A. Josselyn.   E. T. Rowell.   A. Lockhart.
H. Parker.   J. B. Clancy.   W. R. Davis.   J. F. Seavey.

(87)

COMMITTEE ON TAXATION.

Hon. E. B. Crane.   Hon. W. H. Hodgkins.   J. B. L. Bartlett.
                       Hon. J. J. Flynn.
C. G. Washburn, House Chairman.   G. W. Whidden, Clerk.
              Hon. A. L. Harwood, Chairman.
H. H. Bosworth.   G. L. Whitcomb.   S. A. Holton.   F. S Richardson.
J. A. Codman, Jr.   O. T. Brooks.   Z. Talbot.   C. A. Dean

COMMITTEE ON TOWNS.

Hon. H. R. Barber.   Hon. W. H. Cook.   Rufus Howe.   Geo. W. Mellen.
W. S. V. Cooke, House Chairman.   Amos E. Hall, Clerk.
                    Hon. W. L. Bouve, Chairman.
B. Porter, Jr.   Thos. H. Meek.   M. M. Stebbins.   Arthur R. Taft.

COMMITTEE ON WATER SUPPLY.

Hon. W. H. Fairbank.   Hon. W. A. Whittlesey.   W. F. Howard
D. G. Pratt.
G. M. Rice, House Chairman.   G. H. Bartlett, Clerk.
Hon. E. W. Roberts, Chairman.
J. M. Philbrick.   G. F. Williams.   J. A. Montgomery.   John Favor.

COMMITTEE ON WAYS AND MEANS.

Hon. E. W. Roberts.   Hon. J. A. Gallivan.   Hon. W. A. Whittlesey.
Hon. S. W. George.

Albert Clarke, House Chairman.   H. C. Parsons, Clerk.
Hon. J. B. Farley, Chairman.   T. W. Kenefick.
Jas. Thompson.   C. L. Dean.   J. G. Waite.   Almon E. Hall.
A. F. Hayward.   G. H. Carleton.   A. S. Paton.   F. F. Farrar.

HALL OF THE HOUSE OF REPRESENTATIVES.

READING ROOM AND POST OFFICE OF THE HOUSE OF REPRESENTATIVES

VIEW FROM THE CUPOLA TO THE SOUTH.

SERGEANT AT ARMS AND SOME APPOINTEES.

D. T. REMINGTON, T. J. TUCKER, JOHN KINNEAR, JAMES BEATTY, Postmaster.
Senate Door-keeper.   House Door-keeper.   Asst. House Door-keeper.
C. G. DAVIS,   C. W. PHILBRICK,   C. A. LEGG,   L. A. PHILLIPS.
    1st Clerk.   Messenger. Chief Engineer. Doc. Room Messenger.
        CAPT. J. G. B. ADAMS, Sergeant-at-arms.
E. T. POPE.†   H. W. SYKES.†   D. G. GOULD.†   J. H. LOCKE.*
F. A. IRELAND.* A. G. BEAN.* SIDNEY HOLMES.† C. J. TARBELL.† R. J. TAYLOR.
                                                                                Elevator Man.
H. W. MORGAN.§   L. G. MITCHELL.§   C. J. SMITH.¶   E. S. BACKMAN.¶
*Senate Messenger.   †House Messenger.   §Senate Page   ¶House Page.

CORRIDOR OF THE HOUSE OF REPRESENTATIVES.

Main Corridor Between House and Office of Secretary of State.

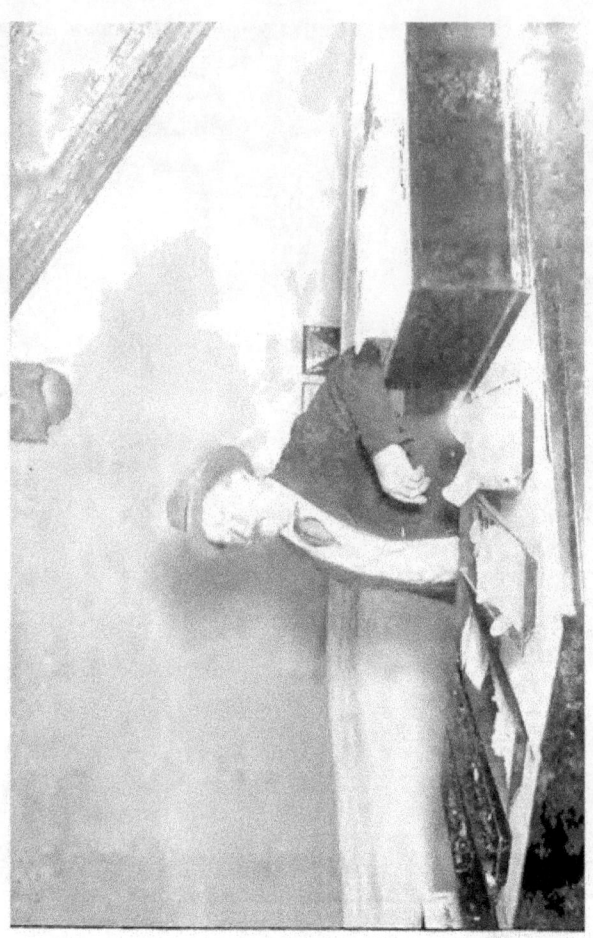

"TOM" MEAGHER, the Veteran of the War of the Rebellion, Who
popular "Candy Man" of the Legislature for, lo, these many

EAST FRONT OF THE STATE HOUSE.

THE OLD STATE HOUSE.

Built in 1748, on site of burned town hall at the head of State Street, Boston

In the foreground occurred the Boston Massacre of March 5, 1770. Been used as State House, City Hall, and Post Office. British troops quartered here, 1768, and General Gage held council of war here before battle of Bunker Hill. Declaration of Independence read from balcony in view; from other end Washington reviewed procession in 1789. Here State Constitution planned and ratified. William Lloyd Garrison took refuge here from mob, October, 1835, it being then used for City Hall.

BIOGRAPHICAL.

BRIEF SKETCHES OF THE LIVES OF THE MEN WHO, IN STATE GOVERNMENT, HELPED SHAPE LEGISLATION IN 1898.

THE GOVERNOR.

His Excellency Roger Wolcott, Republican, of Boston, born in that city July 13, 1847, being a lineal descendant of Oliver Wolcott, one of the signers of the Declaration of Independence. He graduated from Harvard University in the class of 1870, and was class orator. He was a member of Boston common council in 1877-8-9, and the House of Representatives in 1882-3-4, serving on the committees on libraries, labor, and public charitable institutions, and being chairman of the standing House committee on elections. He was the first president of the Republican Club of Massachusetts, is an overseer of Harvard University, and a trustee of Massachusetts General Hospital. Was lieutenant governor in 1893, and was on the committees on pardons, finance, charitable institutions, prisons, military affairs and railroads. On the same committees in 1894, and also on committee on State House extension. On the same committees in 1895 as in 1894, and also on nominations. In 1896 on committees on pardons, finance, charitable institutions, military and naval affairs, railroads, State House, nominations, being chairman of each. By the death of Gov Greenhalge, March 5, the duties of the office of Governor for the rest of the year devolved upon the lieutenant-governor, with the title of "Acting Governor." The unusual conditions of the campaign of 1896, combined with general approval of his administration as "Acting Governor," resulted in his receiving the enormous and unprecedented plurality of 152,542 over George Fred. Williams, the Democratic candidate for Governor, with a majority of 131,344 over all his opponents. And even in the "off year" of 1897, his plurality over his nearest competitor was the unusual one of 85,543.

Vote of the state: John Bascom, Prohibition, 4948; T. C. Brophy, Socialist Labor, 6301; William Everett, Democrat National, 13,879; George Fred. Williams, Democrat, 79,552; Roger Wolcott, Republican, 165,095.

THE LIEUTENANT GOVERNOR.

His Honor Winthrop Murray Crane, Republican, was born in Dalton, where he has lived all his life, April 20, 1853. He was educated in public and private schools. He has always been engaged in the manufacture of paper, his father and grandfather having been engaged in the same business there before him. Although much interested in politics, and always having been an earnest Republican, he has never accepted a nomination for an elective office before his present one. In 1896 he was delegate to the national Republican convention at St. Louis. Chairman of committees on pardons, finance, charitable institutions, prisons, military and naval affairs, railroads, State House, nominations, with Executive Council of 1897, and in the same positions in 1898.

Vote of the state: E. A. Buckland, Socialist Labor, 7379; C. T. Callahan, Democrat, 77,003; J. E. Cotter, Democrat National, 16,202; W. Murray Crane, Republican, 157,106; W. O. Wylie, Prohibition, 6253.

SECRETARY OF THE COMMONWEALTH.

HON. WILLIAM MILO OLIN, of Boston, Republican, is the sixteenth incumbent of the office of Secretary of the Commonwealth since 1710. He is serving his eighth term there. He was born of New England parents in Warrenton, Ga., Sept. 18, 1845, but has been a resident of this state since 1850, and is a graduate of the public schools. He very early entered the office of the Worcester Transcript, starting at the bottom of the ladder as the "devil." He followed that with work at the case until the summer 1862. Then at the age of sixteen, he enlisted in the Thirty-sixth Massachusetts Volunteers and served throughout the war in that organization. Returning to civil life, he devoted some time to study, under the guidance of Rev. Edward Everett Hale, and then joined the reportorial staff of the Boston Advertiser with which paper he was connected for fourteen years, as reporter, editor, and Washington correspondent. In 1897 he was appointed private secretary and military secretary, with the rank of colonel, by Gov. Talbot, and was re-appointed by Gov. Long in 1880, 1881, and 1882. Private secretary to Collector Worthington, Senator Dawes, and Collector Beard; leaving the service of the last named to take up the duties of his present office. He has been lieutenant-colonel and assistant adjutant-general under Gen. Wales, First Brigade, M. V. M., and adjutant-general and inspector-general of the national encampment, G. A. R. Member of Columbia lodge, St. Paul's royal arch chapter, Boston council of Joseph Warren commandery of Masons, all of Boston; also of Massachusetts consistory, 32d degree A. A. S. Rite.

Vote of state: A. W. Barr, Socialist Labor, 8260; C. D. Nash, Democrat, 75,846; William M. Olin, Republican, 157,009; Edwin Sawtell, Prohibition, 5199; B. M. Wolf, Democrat, 11,276.

TREASURER AND RECEIVER-GENERAL.

HON. EDWARD P. SHAW, Republican, of Newburyport, was born in that city, Sept. 1, 1841. He was educated in its public schools. Has always been engaged in business enterprises, especially street railways, and executing large government contracts. In the House of 1881-2, he served on the committee on roads and bridges; and again in 1888-9, on street railways: in the Senate of 1892, he was chairman of committee on street railways, and on committee on banks and banking; in 1893 again chairman of same, and member of banks and banking, insurance, and fisheries and game. Director of First national bank of Newburyport for last 21 years and now its president; also a trustee for many years of the Five Cents savings bank of Newburyport. Chosen state treasurer, April 25, 1895, to fill vacancy caused by resignation of Hon. Henry M. Phillips of Springfield and unanimously renominated in state convention of 1895, and elected by 65,038 majority. Unanimously renominated in state convention, 1896, and elected by 159,923 majority.

Vote of state: G. A. Brown, Socialist Labor, 8595; R. C. Habberly, Prohibition, 5332; Edward P. Shaw, Republican, 153,888; H. P. Tobey, Democrat National, 14,623; T. A. Watson, Democrat, 74,021.

AUDITOR OF ACCOUNTS.

HON. JOHN WHITE KIMBALL, of Fitchburg, Republican, a native of that city, was born Feb. 27, 1828; educated in its public schools. Member of the House of Representatives in 1864, 1865, and 1872, assigned to committee on military affairs each year. Again in House in 1888, 1889, 1890, and 1891, with service on committees on finance and railroads, being chairman of the latter committee in the two last years named; appointed on joint special committee to convey to Congress the resolution relating to couplers and brakes on freight cars; on special committee to investigate the West End R. R. Co. in 1890. He has held these offices: justice of the peace, tax collector, selectman, postmaster, and alderman of Fitchburg; police commissioner of Massachusetts; United States pension agent, Western Massachusetts district; custodian in United States Treasury Department, Washington; commander of the Department of Massachusetts, G. A. R.; before the war, captain and adjutant, Ninth Regiment, M. V. M.; during the war, lieutenant-colonel Fifteenth Massachusetts Volunteers, colonel Fifty-third Massachusetts Volunteers, and brevet brigadier-general United States Volunteers; since the war, colonel Tenth Regiment, M. V. M. A member of the Loyal Legion. He is a real estate agent. Is now serving his sixth term as auditor. Member of Aurora lodge of Masons and Jerusalem commandery, Fitchburg. Is trustee and auditor of Fitchburg sav'ngs bank.

Vote of state: J. Ballam, Socialist Labor, 8190; Harry Douglas, Democrat National, 12,498; John W. Kimball, Republican, 154,316; J. H. Sheldon, Democrat, 74,061; H. M. Small, Prohibition, 4748.

THE ATTORNEY GENERAL.

HON. HOSEA MORRILL KNOWLTON, New Bedford, Republican, born in Durham, Me., May 20, 1847. Educated in Bangor, (Me.) High school, Keene, (N. H.) High school and Powers Institute, Bernardston; Tufts College, class of 1867; Harvard Law School. Admitted to bar, New Bedford, June, 1870. U. S. Register in Bankruptcy 1872-1878, inclusive. City solicitor, 1877. Member of House, 1876-7, committees on insurance, revision of judicial system, chairman of committee on elections. Member of Senate 1878 9, railroad committee. District attorney for Southern District of Massachusetts, 1879 to 1893 inclusive; attorney general 1894-5-6-7-8.

Vote of state: W. Hamlin, Prohibition, 5866; W. Harrison, Socialist Labor, 8115; Hosea M. Knowlton, Republican, 155,048; W. W. McClench, Democrat National, 12,954; J. A. O'Keefe, Democrat, 74,245.

THE EXECUTIVE COUNCIL.

DISTRICT No. 1.

HON. NATHANIEL F. RYDER, Republican, of Middleboro, was born in Middleboro, October 13, 1845, attended the public schools and graduated from Pierce Academy. At eighteen he entered upon work which has been his principal business all his life. He was employed by W. C. Hunneman in their varnish establishment, and at twenty he was a salesman with a big salary for Stimson, Babcock & Livermore. Here he declined a partnership, but subsequently became a member of the firm of Odiorne & Ryder. They were burned out in the great Boston fire. After the great loss by this fire Mr. Ryder began life anew, as it were. The firm of Burbank, Ryder & Damon was formed and exists today, with but a single change, under the name of Burbank & Ryder, doing the largest business of any in the trade in New England, and having factories in Charlestown and Middleboro and stores in Boston and Chicago. The Boston store is at 149 A Milk street. They occupy a most honorable position in the commercial world. Treasurer of the Parlor Pride manufacturing company, also treasurer of the Granite mills. Mr. Ryder cast his first vote for General Grant for president, and has always been a true and loyal Republican. He has never held other public office but has been a generous promoter of the cause for years with his means and has been active in the political clubs and committees, being at present a leading member of the Republican state committee from the Second Plymouth district and chairman of the First district councillor committee. He is treasurer of the Plymouth County club, and a member of the State Republican, Home Market, Middlesex, Algonquin and Norfolk clubs. He has acquired a leading position by association with the prominent party leaders of the state and outside, and was a warm personal friend of Gov. Greenhalge. He is also a Mason of high degree. He was nominated by acclamation and was elected by an almost unanimous vote. On committees on finance, harbors and public lands, military and naval affairs, railroads, nominations in Executive Council of 1896; on pardons, finance, harbors and public lands, railroads, State House and nominations, 1897; on pardons, finance, harbors and public lands (chairman), railroads, State House and nominations, 1898.

Vote of district: Nathaniel F. Ryder, Republican, 19,062; all others, 50.

DISTRICT No. 2.

HON. BENJAMIN S. LOVELL, Republican, of Weymouth, was born in (East) Weymouth, July 10, 1844; educated in the public schools. Enlisted in Co. A, 42d regiment, September 13, 1862, serving in the Department of the Gulf Member of Reynolds post 58 G. A. R., serving six terms as senior vice commander, and for 14 years was successively chosen commander until business matters demanded so much of his time that he was obliged to decline a 15th election. Junior vice commander of the department in 1880, senior vice commander in 1881, and declined the nomination as department commander in 1882. Aide-de-camp to Gen. Robinson, commander in chief of the national encampment in 1886-8; delegate to the national encampment, 1886; member of council of administration, 1887; on staff of Gen. Alger in 1889; on staff of Gen. Palmer, 1892. Member of the staff of Gov. Long 1880-1-2. Delegate to the national Republican conventions of 1884-8-92; Republican presidential elector in 1882. For several years chairman of Weymouth Republican town committee. Member of the House in 1877-8-86-7, on committees on mercantile affairs, railroads, and redistricting the state; an earnest advocate of the Soldiers' Exemption bill in 1886. Member of Senate in 1883, on committees on harbors and public lands, military affairs, Hoosac Tunnel and Troy & Greenfield railroad. Member of Orphans' Hope lodge of Masons, South Shore commandery; Crescent lodge of Odd Fellows Member of the staff of Gov. Greenhalge in 1894-5, with the rank of assistant adjutant-general, resigning when he was chosen to the Council. On committees on harbors and public lands, military and naval affairs, railroads, accounts, and warrants in Council of 1896; on the same committees in the Executive Council of 1897; on same in 1898 (chairman of accounts.)

Vote of district: D. Estes, Democratic National, 2430; Benjamin S. Lovell, Republican, 22,419; G. O. Wentworth, Democrat, 8831.

DISTRICT No. 3.

HON. GEORGE N. SWALLOW, Republican, was born Jan. 2, 1854, in Charlestown (now part of Boston), and was educated in public schools. Been in grocery business since 1872. Member of Ward 5 Republican, and of Republican city committee for past nine years; member Republican state central committee, 1890-91; member of House of Representatives, 1889-91; on committee on harbors and public lands, 1889; chairman of same committee, 1890; and clerk of committee on mercantile affairs, 1891. Candidate for senator from this district, 1892, but was defea ed. Chairman of committee on constitutional amendments, on commitees on cities, water supply, Senate 1894; on committees on pardons, charitable institutions, military and naval affairs, accounts, warrants (chairman), 1898.

Vote of district: J. McSorley, Democrat, 12,171; George N. Swallow, Republican, 20,828.

DISTRICT No. 4

HON. JOHN H. SULLIVAN of Boston, Democrat, was born in Ireland on April 27th, 1848, and was educated in the national schools. After coming to

Boston he took a business course at Comer's Commercial College and immediately entered the shipping business at Boston, in which business he was most successful for a period of 30 years, retiring about a year ago in order to devote his time to the banking business. He is president and manager of the Columbia Trust Company; a trustee and chairman of the investment committee of the Sumner savings bank. Both of these institutions owe their existence and success to his perseverance and energy. Mr. Sullivan is a large real estate owner; among other property owned by him is the well known Lyceum hall on Maverick square, East Boston, the Columbia bank and office building. Mr. Sullivan allowed the use of his name for the common council of Boston in the fall of 1883, and was elected by the largest vote given any one for that office up to that time; he served in that body in 1884-5 and in the board of aldermen of 1886-7 and 1891-2, being the senior member during the years 1891-2; he was on important committees. He was elected to the state Senate in 1888 after one of of the greatest contests in his district ever entered into for that office. He served on the committees on liquor law and public service. He was delegate at large from Massachusetts to the 1862 national Democratic convention in Chicago. He is a sinking fund commissioner of the city of Boston, has been a delegate a large to all Democratic state conventions for the last 15 years; and has been treasurer of the Democratic state committee of Massachusetts and the Democratic city committee of Boston for many years. Mr. Sullivan was elected to the Executive Council for 1895-6, and was doubtless really elected for 1997, but because the "cross" on 340 ballots was not within the space required he was declared not elected. He was however, again elected for 1898 by the largest majority ever given in the district for that office. In this office Mr. Sullivan served on committees on pardons, harbors and public lands, prisons, railroads, and warrants in Executive Council of 1895; on pardons, finance, harbors and public lands (ch), prisons, railroads, and State House, 1896; and on committees on pardons, harbors and public lands, charitable institutions, railroads, and State House, 1898.

Vote of district: S. Ruffin, Republican, 12,664; John H. Sullivan, Democrat, 21,591.

DISTRICT No. 5.

HON. HORACE H. ATHERTON, Republican, of Saugus, was born Oct. 23, 1847, in that town; educated in public schools and Lynn High school, class of 1864. In 1865 became clerk for Oliver Breed, lumber business, now carried on under firm name of Guilford, Atherton & Co.. Mr Atherton, being junior partner. Been auditor, assessor, selectman. House of Representatives, 1888, 20th Essex district, committee on banks and banking; also, 1889. committee on prisons, and special committee to represent state at Ohio centennial at Columbus. Republican state committee. 1893-4. Director in Saugus Mutual fire insurance company; secretary Republican town committee. Masons; Odd Fellows. Chairman committee on towns, on parishes and religious societies, street railways. Senate of 1895; chairman of committee on towns, and on printing, and street railways, Senate of 1896. On committees on harbors and public lands, charitable institutions, prisons, nominations, warrants, 1898.

Vote of district: Horace H. Atherton, Republican, 19,536; J. L. Libby, Democrat National, 1669; D. H. Maguire, Democrat, 7,838.

DISTRICT No. 6.

HON. ELISHA HERMANN SHAW, Republican, merchant, of Chelmsford, was born in that town, Sept. 29, 1847, in North Chelmsford. He received his education in the public schools, and at Comer's Commercial College in Boston. He has been a brass molder, second hand in a woolen mill, but is now proprietor of a general store at North Chelmsford. He has been postmaster at North Chelmsford for some twenty-five years, and has served as selectman, assessor and overseer of the poor. He is captain of Troop F. cavalry of the state militia. In the Masonic fraternity he has been worshipful master of William North lodge of Masons, high priest of Mt. Horeb chapter of royal arch Masons, and thrice illustrious master of Ahasuerus council of Royal and Select Masons, all of the city of Lowell, and in 1890, 1891 and 1892 he was district deputy grand master for the Eleventh Masonic district. Ill. 2d lieutenant commander of Massachusetts consistory A. & A. S. Rite, 1892 3-4. Member of board of trustees of Lowell Five Cent savings bank of Lowell. In 1884 member of the House, serving on committee on insurance. Chairman of the committee on military affairs, and member of committee on public health, in Senate of 1893; chairman of committees on military affairs, and printing; and on street railways in Senate of 1894. On committees on finance, military, and naval affairs, State House, accounts in Executive Council of 1897; on committees on finance, prisons, military and naval affairs, State House, accounts, 1898.

Vote of district: Elisha H. Shaw, Republican, 25,710; all others, 40.

DISTRICT No. 7.

HON. ALLEN L. JOSLIN, Republican, of Oxford was born in Thompson, Conn., Aug. 30, 1833, and was educated in the public schools. At 17 he came to Oxford and entered the shoe factory of L. B. Corbin and worked practically at every part of boot and shoe making. He saved his earnings and on becoming proficient as a workman he began business for himself in 1857, when 24 years old. In 1860 he formed a co-partnership with his former employers under the style of L. B. Corbin & Co. In 1871 Mr. Joslin built a factory of his own and admitted into partnership his brother. The firm of A. L. Joslin & Co, has become one of the best known shoe manufacturing firms in Massachusetts. Mr. Joslin has filled the office of town treasurer for fifteen consecutive years; has been selectman, member of the school committee, and president of the Oxford national bank since 1881; and also has filled many positions of trust in a personal capacity. He was elected a member of the House of Representatives in 1885. John Q. A. Brackett was speaker and appointed him a member of the committee on banks and banking. In 1886 he was elected to the Senate, and in this body he was chairman of the joint standing committee on banks and banking, and was also on the committees on State House and claims. He is a member of the Home Market Club and Republican Club, of the Boston Art Club and of the Boston Merchants' Association. On committees on finance, pardons, prisons, and State House in the Executive Council of 1897, and on pardons, finance, prisons, railroads, and State House in 1898.

Vote of district: John Gregson, Democrat, 9194; Allen L. Joslin, Republican, 18,910.

DISTRICT No. 8.

HON. WILLIAM B. PLUNKETT, Republican, was born in Adams, where he has resided ever since, April 2, 1852. He was educated in its public schools and in Munro Collegiate Institute of Elbridge, N. Y. In 1871 he became partner in the well known firm of Plunkett & Wheeler, cotton warp manufacturers After the death of Mr. Wheeler, the firm united with that of W. B. Plunkett & Sons, which is still continued, the partners now being the subject of this sketch and his brother, Mr. Charles T. Plunkett. He has always been prominently identified with every movement for the advancement and prosperity of the town, not only by thought and word but by many deeds as well. He is treasurer of the Greylock Mills of North Adams, of the Berkshire Cotton Manufacturing Co. of Adams; president of the Greylock national bank of Adams, director of the Berkshire Mutual life insurance company and of the Berkshire Mutual fire insurance company of Pittsfield, and holds similar positions in other equally prominent corporations. In 1892 he was a delegate to the Republican national convention, and in 1896 he was in close touch with the Republican national committee. He enjoys the distinction of being "the original McKinley man" in Massachusetts, and is an intimate friend of the president. In 1897, he was appointed on the Government board of visitors at West Point. At the annual meeting of the Home Market Club in 1897 he was chosen its president. Having been elected to the Governor's Executive Council, he was appointed on the committees on finance, harbors and public lands, prisons, military and naval affairs, 1898.

Vote of district: William B. Plunkett, Republican, 22,426; E. J. Tierney, Democrat, 13,266.

Private Secretary.—JAMES M. PERKINS, Republican, of Cambridge, was born in Tamworth, N. H., April 17, 1868; educated in Somerville High school, and Harvard College, class of 1892, and Harvard Law School, class of 1895. Is a lawyer. Clerk of judiciary committee of the United States Senate in the second session of the 52d Congress. Member of St. John's lodge of Masons of Boston, of St. Paul's chapter, and of Boston commandery of Knights Templar.

Executive Secretary.—EDWARD F. HAMLIN, Republican, of Newton, was born in Plainfield, Mass., in 1844; removed to Northampton in 1857. Sept., 1862, enlisted as a private in Co. 1, 52d regiment, Massachusetts Volunteers; promoted to first sergeant; served in Department of the Gulf; mustered out at expiration of service, Aug. 14, 1863. In 1867 was elected first lieutenant and captain, Co. H, 2d regiment, Massachusetts Volunteer Militia; was appointed to a clerkship in the adjutant-general's office by Gov. Washburn in 1874; in 1877 appointed clerk of the Governor and Council by Gov. Rice and held that position to March 1, 1898, when the title of the office was changed to "Executive Secretary."

THE SENATE

THE PRESIDENT.

HON. GEORGE EDWIN SMITH, Republican, of Everett, was born in New Hampton, Belknap county, N. H., April 5, 1849. Fitted for college at Literary Institution New Hampton; graduated at Bates College, class of 1873. Studied law in the office of Senator William P. Frye, Lewiston, Me.; admitted to the bar of Suffolk county, May, 1875; practiced there since. Moved to Everett in 1878; trustee of public library since 1880; member of school committee; chairman of committee to procure city charter in 1892; city solicitor in 1893-4. Chosen by alumni one of the overseers of Bates College in 1879 and was elected in 1884 and continues to be one of the Board of Fellows. Member of Palestine lodge of Masons of Everett. Member of House of Representatives in 1883-4 from eighth Middlesex district (Malden and Everett); served on committees on education, taxation, and roads and bridges (ch). Committee on judiciary; and on bills in 3d reading, (ch), and liquor law in Senate of 1897. Chosen president of Senate of 1898 by a unanimous vote.

Vote of district: G. E. Carbee, Democrat, 1219; George E. Smith, Republican, 4550.

BRISTOL COUNTY.

First District.—*Attleboro, Berkley, Easton, Mansfield, North Attleboro, Norton, Raynham, Rehoboth, Seekonk, Taunton.*—HON. WILLIAM R. BLACK,

Republican, of Taunton, was born in Prince Edward's Island, Aug. 23, 1830; educated in the public schools. Went to Taunton in 1852. Was in Co. G, 4th regiment of militia, and when the war broke out went with that company to Fortress Monroe in answer to the President's first call for 75,000 men. Was one of the "Minute Men", three months' service. Was in the first fight of the war at Big Bethel, Va., in June, 1861; re-enlisted with his company at the expiration of service. Was 1st lieutenant of Co. G.; promoted to captain of Co. F. Ordered to the Department of the Gulf, under General Banks, in 19th Army Corps, and went through most of the marches and battles of the department. Was a cotton planter in North Carolina for four years from the close of the war, and worked some of the first free negroes in that state. Since 1869 has been a contractor, paver and road builder in Taunton. Member of Post 3. G. A. R; St. Marks, R. A. chapter, King David lodge, F. & A. M.; Knights of Honor; Home Market Club, Old Colony Historical Society. Superintendent of streets of Taunton, from 1891 to 1895 when he declined further service. Chairman of nominating committee of Bristol County agricultural society; member of Taunton board of trade. Member of House in 1872-3, committees on prisons and bills in third reading. Member of Senate 1897, chairman committee on labor, and on constitutional amendments, and roads and bridges. On committees on printing (ch), constitutional amendments, roads and bridges, 1898.

Vote of district: William R Black, Republican, 3627; all others, 3.

Second District.—Dighton, Fall River, Somerset, Swanzey—HON. WILLIAM MORAN, Democrat, of Fall River, was born in Manchester, England, Sept. 6, 1855; educated in the public schools of Fall River. Is a barber. Chairman of Democratic city committee in 1895-6. Member of the House of 1894-5, serving on the committee on federal relations in 1894, and on labor in 1895. On committees on election laws, insurance, and labor in Senate of 1897. On committees on insurance, labor, public charitable institutions, 1898.

Vote of district: William Moran, Democrat, 5238; J. O. Neill, Republican, 4060.

Third District.—Acushnet, Dartmouth, Fairhaven, Freetown, New Bedford, Westport.—HON. RUFUS A. SOULE of New Bedford, Republican, was born in Mattapoisett, March 16, 1839; educated in the public schools. Enlisted in Co. E, Third regiment, in Sept., 1862; mustered out in June, 1863. Past commander of post 190 G. A. R. Member of Loyal Legion. President of Hathaway, Soule & Harrington, incorporated, shoe manufacturers; president of the Dartmouth cotton mills, and director in the City and Bristol cotton mills also; vice president of the New Bedford safe deposit, loan and trust company; president of the Acushnet co-operative bank, and director of the New Bedford co-operative bank; director of the W. S. Hill electric manufacturing company. Member of the Middlesex club. Member of common council five years and its president in 1874. Member of Star in the East lodge of Masons, of Adoniram chapter, and of Sutton commandery of Knights Templar. Trustee of New Bedford Five Cents savings bank; director of New Bedford, Middleboro & Brockton street railway company. Member of House 1878-9, serving on committee on railroads. Chairman of committee on banks and banking, and on committees on drainage, and railroads; also on committee to redistrict the state, in Senate of 1896; chairman of committee on railroads, and on printing, and State House, 1897. On committees on railroads (chairman,) banks and banking, State House, 1898.

Vote of district: C. T. Luce, Democrat, 736; Rufus A. Soule, Republican, 3402.

ESSEX COUNTY.

First District.—Wards 1, 2, 3, 4, 5, 7 of Lynn, Nahant, Swampscott.—HON. JOSIAH CHASE BENNETT of Lynn, Republican, was born in Sandwich, N. H., May 6, 1835; educated in the public schools. Came to Danvers at 16 and learned the shoe-making trade by working at the bench. Then he engaged in the manufacture of silk hats in Boston, and in photography for some years. In 1865 he became connected with the American Shoe Tip Company of Boston. After spending four years with this company, which he succeeded in building up from a yearly deficit to one upon a large and prosperous dividend paying basis, he removed to Lynn and began manufacturing shoes, where his house (J. C. Bennett & Barnard) was very successful for many years and became the recognized leaders of ladies' fine shoes and slippers in the country, if not in the world, their product finding a ready market in all the large towns and cities in every state and territory in the Union. He continued to prosper until the great fire of 1889, when he retired from the shoe business and has since been engaged in looking after his real estate interests. In 1885 he was a member of the Senate, serving on the committees on prisons and labor. Delegate to the national Republican convention at Minneapolis in 1892, and has always been prominent in politics. The originator of the "North Shore" route for the state highway, from Boston to Newburyport, he has spent much time in securing its promotion. Chairman of committees on roads and bridges, and drainage; and on committee on harbors and public lands, 1898.

Vote of district: D. B. Beard, Democratic National, 171; Josiah C. Bennett, Republican, 3972; C. E. Bishop, Prohibition, 184; C. A. Taber, Democrat, 1413.

Second District.—Beverly, Danvers, Marblehead, Salem.—HON. JOHN D. H. GAUSS, Republican, was born in Salem, Jan. 4, 1861; educated in public schools. Printer, and publisher of Salem Observer, a weekly local newspaper. Ex-President of Young Men's Republican club. On school committee seven years. Past grand of Fraternity lodge of Odd Fellows; past high priest of Salem encampment; member of Starr King lodge of Masons; also of Naumkeag tribe of Red Men. On committee on railroads, in House of 1894. House chairman of committee on public charitable institutions, and ranking member on committee on railroads, 1895; House chairman of committee on public charitable institutions, and on railroads, 1896. Chairman of committee on fisheries and game, and on public charitable institutions, and street railways in Senate of 1897. On committees on public charitable institutions (chairman), bills in 3d reading, parishes and religious societies, 1898.

Vote of district: John D. H Gauss, Republican, 4125; F. L. Wadden, Democrat, 2148.

Third District.—Essex, Gloucester, Hamilton, Ipswich, Manchester, Newbury, Newburyport, Rowley, Wenham.—HON. CHARLES O. BAILEY, of Newbury, Republican, was born in that town, Jan. 24, 1863; educated in Putnam Free School of Newburyport and Bryant & Stratton's commercial college of Boston. In the grocery business. Selectman for 1892 3-4-5; member of school committee 1888-97, inclusive. Member of Charles C. Dame lodge of Masons of Georgetown. Member of Junior Order American Mechanics; March 30, 1896, elected an alternate delegate from the 6th congressional district to the Republican national convention at St. Louis. Clerk of committee on public service, 1896; also clerk of special committee on redistricting the state; on committee on public charitable institutions in House of 1897; on committees on fisheries and game (chairman), engrossed bills, agriculture, street railways, 1898.

Vote of district: Charles O. Bailey, Republican, 3641; Albert Currier, Democrat, 1032; J. F. Young, Democrat National, 360.

Fourth District.—Amesbury, Georgetown, Groveland, Haverhill, Merrimac, Salisbury, West Salisbury.—HON. SAMUEL WESLEY GEORGE, Republican, was born in Meredith, N. H., April 26, 1862. His father, a member of Co. I, 12th New Hampshire, having died in January, 1863, near Falmouth, Va., his mother moved to Concord, N. H., and thence to Northwood, N. H., where he was educated in public schools and seminary of the latter town. After serving two years in a grocery and post-office removed to Haverhill early in 1883, and was identified with its shoe industry until 1894, and since then has been agent and manager of the Merrimac Valley steamboat company. Member of common council in 1888-89-90, serving as its president the latter year. Member of House, 1894, clerk of committee on labor; House chairman of committee on public service and on committees on finance and expenditures, 1895; House chairman of committee on public service, and on ways and means, 1896, also member of the committee making arrangements for the state memorial service to the late Gov. Greenhalge, and a member of the special committee to investigate the official acts of the Norfolk county commissioners in connection with building the new court house at Dedham; House chairman of committee on libraries, and on ways and means, 1897; on committees on public service (chairman), ways and means, election laws, 1898.

Vote of district: Samuel W. George, Republican, 3234; T. Kelley, Democrat, 1167; G. A. Kelly, Socialist Labor, 389; H. G. Leslie, Democrat National, 281.

Fifth District.—Andover, Boxford, Lawrence, Methuen, North Andover, Topsfield.—HON. JOSEPH J. FLYNN, Democrat, of Lawrence was born in Ireland, May 1, 1862, came to Lawrence 1863; educated in public schools; worked in mills. Treasurer of Lawrence Opera House, manager and part owner of Lawrence bill posting company. In House of 1895, committee on county estimates; 1896, committees on manufactures, elections, and special committee on redistricting the state. On committees on counties, education, and taxation, 1898.

Vote of district: Harry R. Dow, Republican, 3937; Joseph J. Flynn, Democrat, 5311; E. Searle, Prohibition, 140.

HAMPDEN COUNTY.

First District.—Brimfield, Holland, Monson, Springfield, Wales, Wilbraham.—HON. WILLIAM W. LEACH of Palmer, Republican, was born in Monson, Feb. 22, 1856; educated in the public schools, Monson Academy, and Tufts College class of 1880. Is a lawyer. Member of Thomas lodge, Hampden chapter, and Washington council, and Springfield Commandery of Masons. Member of House in 1889, on committees on labor (House chairman), rules, and special committee to investigate the publication of the Province Laws. Chairman of committees on counties, and labor; and on probate and insolvency, 1898.

Vote of district: William W. Leach, Republican, 4691; A. H. Sherwin, Democrat, 2490.

Second District.—Agawam, Chicopee, East Longmeadow, Granville, Holyoke, Longmeadow, Ludlow, Montgomery, Southwick, Tolland, West Springfield, Westfield.—HON. WILLIAM B. MAHONEY of Westfield, Democrat, was born in Bath, Me., Dec. 5, 1857; educated in the public schools. Is in the cigar business. Member of Division 3 of Ancient Order of Hibernians, of Metacomet tribe of Red Men, and of Whip City council of Knights of Columbus. On committees on parishes and religious societies, prisons, and public health, 1898.

Vote of district: D. H. Ives, Republican, 4138; William B. Mahoney, Democrat, 4184.

MIDDLESEX COUNTY.

First District.—Ashland, Framingham, Holliston, Hopkinton, Natick, Newton, Sherborn, Watertown, Weston.—HON. ALBERT L. HARWOOD, Republican was born in Hardwick, Sept. 10, 1847; educated in public schools and Williston Seminary. Taught Lincoln grammar school, Fall River, 1872-3-4-5, then Mason grammar school of Newton Centre, 1876-90, inclusive. Is a lawyer with an office in Boston. On Newton school committee, 1891-2-3. Member of Newton Republican ward and city committee, 1893-4-5. Masons; Knights Templar. On committees on probate and insolvency, finance, and expenditures in House of 1895; House chairman of committee on probate and insolvency, on ways and means, and House chairman of recess committee on conduct of Boston caucuses, 1896; chairman of committee on constitutional amendments, also of committee on counties, and on committee on railroads in Senate of 1897. On committees on taxation (chairman), libraries, railroads, 1898.

Vote of district: C. E. Farrington, Democrat, 2908; Albert L. Harwood, Republican, 5340.

Second District.—Wards 1, 2, 3, 4, 5, of Cambridge.—HON. FREDERICK W. DALLINGER, Republican, was born in Cambridge, Oct. 2, 1871; educated in public schools, and at Harvard College, graduating in class of 1893, at head of his class, receiving highest honors in political science. In 1894 received degree of A. M. and in 1897 that of L. L. B. from the same University. While in Harvard was president of the Harvard Union and one of the originators of the Harvard-Yale joint debates, and one of the Harvard speakers at both debates in New Haven, in 1892 and 1893. Member of Phi Beta Kappa Society. Member of the Suffolk bar and also tutor in Harvard University. President of Cambridge Young Men's Republican club, and secretary of Cambridge Republican city committee, 1893-4. Member of Massachusetts and Middlesex clubs. Clerk of committee on election laws, and on committee on taxation, in House of 1894; chairman of House committee on county estimates, and on committee on metropolitan affairs, 1895. Chairman of committees on counties, and engrossed bills; also on committee on metropolitan affairs, 1896; chairman of committee on metropolitan affairs, and on counties, and probate and insolvency, 1897. On committees on metropolitan affairs (chairman), constitutional amendments, counties, 1898.

Vote of district: H. Bird, Democrat, 2275; Frederick W. Dallinger, Republican, 4018.

Third District.—Arlington, Belmont, Somerville.—HON. WILLIAM H. HODGKINS of Somerville, Republican, was born in Charlestown (now part of Boston), June 9, 1840; educated in the public schools. Enlisted July 22, 1862, in Co. B, 36th regiment and served in Virginia, Mississippi and Tennessee. Promoted to 2d lieutenant, 1st lieutenant, captain, brevet major; mustered out June 8, 1865. Member of Willard C. Kinsley post No. 139, G. A. R., and of Loyal Legion; on staff of commander-in-chief of 1895-6. For 21 years in the service of the public institutions of Boston; since 1887, trustee of the Ballardvale mills. Member of common council 1873, its president in 1874; mayor 1892-3-4-5. On committees on harbors and public lands (chairman), street railways, taxation, 1898.

Vote of district: C. K Cutter, Democrat, 1397; William H. Hodgkins, Republican, 4288.

Fifth District.—Lexington, Lincoln, Marlboro, Sudbury, Waltham, Wayland, Winchester.—HON. HENRY PARSONS, Republican, of Marlboro, was born in New York city, Feb. 2, 1841; educated in public and private schools. Is a manufacturer of machinery, elevators, engines, and various kinds of foundery work. Enlisted as 2d lieutenant, Aug. 2, 1862, in Co H, 148th New York regiment and served in the Army of the Potomac and of the James; wounded four times; promoted to major; mustered out, June 29, 1865. Member of John A. Rawlins post 43 G. A. R., having held all the offices and being past commander. Member of Marlboro common council in 1891-2, and of the aldermen in 1893-4. Marshal of United Brethren lodge of Masons, and of Trinity commandery of

Knights Templar Chairman of committee on federal relations, and on banks
and banking, and military affairs in Senate of 1897. On committees on federal
relations (chairman), banks and banking, drainage, 1898.
Vote of district: W. V. Hyde, Democrat, 1977; Henry Parsons, Republican, 4555; W. C. Waitt, Democrat National, 636.

Sixth District.—Acton, Ashby, Ayer, Bedford, Billerica, Boxborough, Burlington, Carlisle, Concord, Dunstable, Groton, Hudson, Littleton, Wards 5, 9 of Lowell, Maynard, Pepperell, Reading, Shirley, Stow, Tewksbury, Townsend, Tyngsborough, Westford, Wilmington—HON. WILLIAM H. BRIGHAM, Republican, of Hudson, was born Feb. 1, 1863, in Marlboro; educated in the public
schools. Is a shoe manufacturer. On board of selectmen six years, being chairman of the board four years; director of the Hudson national bank, and vice
president of the Hudson savings bank; vice president of board of trade. Member
of Doric lodge of Masons of Houghton royal arch chapter; Trinity commandery of
Knights Templar; No 32, Aleppo Temple, A. A. O N. M. S.; of Royal Arcanum; of local tribe of Red Men; and of Middlesex club. Major and assistant
inspector general of rifle practice of 1st brigade staff. In House of Representatives 1892, on committee of military affairs, and House chairman of banks and
banking in 1893; on special committee to Chicago at dedication of World's Fair
buildings in 1892 and also at "Massachusetts Day" the following year; on special
committee to attend Gen. Butler's funeral in 1893. Chairman of committee on
military affairs, and on committees on education, and towns in Senate of 1897.
On committees on military affairs (chairman), rules, railroads, 1898.
Vote of district: William H. Brigham, Republican, 4290, A. Fisher, Democrat, 2250.

Seventh District.—Chelmsford, Dracut, Wards. 1, 2, 3, 4, 6, 7, 8 of Lowell.—
HON. GEORGE E. PUTNAM, Republican, of Lowell, was born in Croydon, N. H.,
Feb 9, 1851, educated in its public schools. Been engaged in wholesale produce business, 207 Market street, Lowell, for the last 18 years. Member of Pentucket lodge of Masons; and Pilgrim Commandery of Knights Templar; of Lowell
lodge and Monomake encampment of Odd Fellows; of Lowell council of Ancient
Order United Workmen, and of Red Men; also of the Highland and County
clubs and of Martin Luthers, Lowell. Director in Middlesex safe deposit and
trust company, of Lowell. Alderman in 1888-9; water commissioner four years,
term expiring in 1897. Committee on cities in House of 1895; on same committee, 1896. Chairman of committee on cities, and on federal relations and public
service in Senate of 1897. On committees on cities (chairman), agriculture, printing, public service, 1898.
Vote of district; E. D. McVey, Democrat, 3513; George E. Putnam, Republican, 4602.

*Middlesex-Essex District.—Ward 6 of Lynn, Lynnfield, Middleton, North
Reading, Peabody, Saugus, Stoneham, Wakefield, Woburn.*—HON. CHARLES F.
WOODWARD, Republican, of Wakefield, was born in that town, Nov. 19, 1852;
educated in the public schools and a Boston commercial college. For 20 years
was a manufacturer of shoe tools and machinery. For the last ten years engaged
in constructing and managing electric roads. President of the Woburn & Reading, the Mystic Valley, the Wakefield & Stoneham and other street railway companies; formerly president of the Wakefield board of trade, and a vice president
of the state board of trade. Member of the Republican state central committee
in 1891-2. He was for 15 years an assessor and chairman of the board all but
two years Tax collector from 1883 to 1897. Member of Golden Rule lodge of
Masons; and of the A. O. U. W. Member of the House in 1887, on committees
on street railways, and military affairs; in 1888, chairman of military affairs, and
clerk of street railways; in 1889, chairman of street railways, and on federal

relations: in the recess of 1887, chairman of special committee on armories, on report of which the great state armories were built in the various cities; in the recess of 1888, chairman of special committee on soldiers' records. In Aug. 1869, joined Co. A,6th regiment, Richardson Light Guards; private, corporal, sergeant, 1st sergeant, 2d lieutenant, 1st lieutenant, captain, major, lieutenant colonel; elected colonel March 4, 1898, and now holds said office. Answered call of President McKinley for volunteers in the war between Spain and the United States, was with his regiment in camp at South Framingham, and left May 20, at the head of his regiment for "the front," passing through Baltimore, where the regiment was received with great enthusiasm, May 21. A contributing member of the G. A. R Chairman of committee on towns; and on insurance and military affairs in Senate of 1897. On committees on manufactures (chairman), metropolitan affairs, military affairs, 1898.

Vote of district: I. E. Graves, Democrat, 2939; Charles F. Woodward, Republican, 4750.

NORFOLK COUNTY.

First District.—Braintree, Canton, Holbrook, Hyde Park, Milton, Quincy, Randolph, Weymouth.—HON. JAMES H. FLINT, of Weymouth, Republican, was born in Middleton, June 25, 1852; educated in public schools and Phillips Academy of Andover, valedictorian of class of 1872; Harvard College 1876; Boston University Law School, 1881. Principal of Marblehead High school 1876-80. One year in New York city law office. Admitted to Suffolk bar, 1882; practiced in Boston, Weymouth and Quincy since. Author of "Flint on Trusts and Trustees;" editor of "Lewin on Trusts;" and has done a good deal of literary work of various kinds. On school committee of Weymouth last eight years. Secretary of Republican league of Massachusetts in campaign of 1888. Special justice of district court of eastern Norfolk at Quincy several years. Past grand chancellor and grand representative in Knights of Pythias; Delta lodge of Masons, Pentalpha chapter South Shore commandery; New England Order of Protection, and supreme representative. Trustee of Weymouth savings bank, director of South Shore co-operative bank, member of Boston Bar Association. Chairman of Republican town committee since 1895. On committees on street railways, and probate and insolvency in House of 1894. House chairman of committee on street railways and on probate and insolvency, 1895; same positions, 1896. Chairman of committee on insurance; and on probate and insolvency, and on ways and means in Senate of 1897. On committee on insurance (chairman), judiciary, education, 1898.

Vote of district: H. O. Apthorp, Democrat National, 544; James H. Flint, Republican, 4830; T. R. Newell, Democrat, 1957.

Second District.—Avon, Bellingham, Brookline, Dedham, Dover, Foxborough, Franklin, Medfield, Medway, Millis, Needham, Norfolk, Norwood, Sharon, Stoughton, Walpole, Wellesley, Wrentham, Westwood.—HON. FRED HOMER WILLIAMS, of Brookline, Republican, was born in Foxboro, Jan. 7, 1857; educated in the public schools, and Brown University class of 1877. Is a lawyer. Member of Beth-horon lodge of Masons, Lomia lodge of Odd Fellows, and East Medway Grange Patrons of Husbandry. Member of the House of 1883-4, on committee on bills in 3d reading (chairman), 1883, and insurance, (chairman) 1884. On committees on mercantile affairs (chairman), judiciary, rules. 1898.

Vote of district: H. H. Francis, Democrat, 1249; Fred H. Williams, Republican, 4404; G. S. Winslow, Democrat National, 889.

PLYMOUTH COUNTY.

First District.—Abington, Carver, Cohasset (Norfolk County), Duxbury, East Bridgewater, Halifax, Hanover, Hanson, Hingham, Hull, Kingston,

Marshfield, Norwell, Pembroke, Plympton, Rockland, Scituate, Whitman.—
HON. WALTER LINCOLN BOUVE, of Hingham, Republican, was born in Boston,
Oct. 28, 1849; educated in public and private schools, Massachusetts Institute
of Technology, 1874, and Harvard Law School, 1879. A civil engineer until
1877; counselor at law since 1880. Special justice of the 2d district court of
Plymouth since 1885; commissioner for Georgia since 1889; assistant district
attorney for southeastern district, 1890-1; 1st lieutenant First Corps of Cadets
since 1890. Chairman Republican town committee; chairman Republican district committee. Clerk of committee on taxation, and on ways and means in
House of 1896; chairman of engrossed bills, and on judiciary in House of 1897;
On committees on towns (chairman), military affairs, probate and insolvency,
public health, 1898. Appointed by President McKinley on staff of Gen. Fitz
Hugh Lee, 1898, as assistant adjutant general with rank of captain.

Vote of district: Walter L. Bouve, Republican, 3037; A. Shanahan, Democrat, 1195.

Second District:—*Bridgewater, Brockton, Lakeville, Marion, Mattapoisett,
Middleboro, Rochester, Wareham, West Bridgewater.*—HON. LOYED E. CHAMBERLAIN, of Brockton, Republican, was born in Plympton, Jan. 30, 1857; moved
to Brockton (then North Bridgewater) in 1859; educated in the public schools,
and Boston University Law School class of 1879. Is a lawyer. Justice of the
Brockton police court since 1885, city solicitor of Brockton 1891-2 3 4, school
committee since 1887, president of board of trade since it was established in
1896. Senior warden of Paul Revere lodge of Masons, member of Massasoit
lodge of Odd Fellows, of Fraternal lodge of Good Templars, of Brookville Grange
of Patrons of Husbandry, and of Banner lodge of N. E. O. P. On committees
on bills in 3d reading (chairman), cities, insurance, 1898.

Vote of district: Loyed E. Chamberlain, Republican, 3312; E. Cushman,
Democrat, 1355.

SUFFOLK COUNTY.

First District.—*Chelsea, Revere, Winthrop, Ward 1 of Boston.*—HON.
ERNEST W. ROBERTS, Republican, of Chelsea, born in East Madison, Me., Nov.
22, 1858; Chelsea schools; Highland Military Academy, Worcester; Boston
University Law School, 1881. Lawyer. Chelsea common council in 1887 88.
Masons. Committee on water supply in House of 1894; House chairman of liquor law, clerk of committee on water supply, chairman of special committee on
history of the "Ancient Codfish," 1895. House chairman of liquor law, and
clerk of water supply, 1896. Chairman of committee on water supply; and on
drainage, and ways and means in Senate of 1897. On committees on water supply (chairman), ways and means, drainage, 1898.

Vote of district: E. M. Cunningham, Democrat, 2157; Ernest W. Roberts,
Republican, 4758.

Second District.—*Wards 3, 4, 5 of Boston, Ward 3 of Cambridge.*—HON.
DAVID B. SHAW, Democrat, born in Boston, (Charlestown) Aug. 20, 1870; public
schools and Boston University. Furniture polisher; now law student in office of
Hon. Joseph J. Corbett and Boston University Law School. Member of Knights
of Columbus. Committee on metropolitan affairs, 1896; clerk of same, 1897.
Elected at a special election, March 29, to fill the vacancy caused by the death of
Hon. James E. Hayes, receiving 2036 votes to 74 scattering. On committees on
libraries and liquor law.

Third District.—*Wards 2, 6, 8 of Boston.*—HON. DANIEL D. ROURKE,
Democrat, of Boston, was born in that city 27 years ago; public schools. Paper
hanger. Common council 1893-4. House of 1895, committee on printing; 1896,
counties; 1897, street railways; also, 1895, House chairman committee on dedica-

tion of John Boyle O'Reilly monument; 1896, committees on dedication of Robert G. Shaw memorial, on congressional district lines. On committees on federal relations, manufactures, and printing in Senate of 1898.

Vote of district: W. J. Donovan, Democrat Bryan N. P., 1059; W. W. Farr, Republican, 1211; Daniel D. Rourke, Democrat, 4081; S. L. Silverman, Republican Citizens N. P., 771.

Fourth District.—*Wards 7, 9, 17 of Boston.*—HON. CHARLES I. QUIRK of Boston, Democrat, was born in Boston, Aug. 15, 1871; educated in its public schools, and Boston College, class of 1891. Professor at Boston College one year; studied law at Boston University Law School, being in class of 1895 of that institution; admitted to Suffolk bar, Dec. 12, 1894. Committees on judiciary, and probate and insolvency, 1895; probate and insolvency, and elections, 1896; probate and insolvency, and election laws in House of 1897; on committees on judiciary, engrossed bills, election laws, 1898.

Vote of district: J. E. Gill Republican, 2225; Charles I. Quirk, Democrat, 4347.

Fifth District.—*Wards 10, 12, 18 of Boston.*—HON. WILLIAM W. TOWLE, Republican of Boston, was born in Fryeburg, Me., Aug. 21, 1860; educated in Fryeburg academy, and in Bowdoin College, class of 1881; and in Boston University Law School, class of 1884. Is a lawyer. Member of common council in 1889 90. Member of Wm. Parkman lodge of Masons of Winchester. Member of House in 1895, on committee on probate and insolvency and chairman of the former committee; and on bills in 3d reading, and metropolitan affairs in Senate of 1897. On committees on probate and insolvency (chairman), labor, metropolitan affairs, 1898.

Vote of district: J. W. Palmer, Democrat, 2565; William W. Towle, Republican, 3969.

Sixth District.—*Wards 13, 14, 15, of Boston.*—HON. JAMES A GALLIVAN, Democrat, was born in South Boston, Oct. 22, 1866, and has always resided in Ward 13. Graduated from Lawrence grammar school and Boston Latin school, receiving the Franklin medal at graduation. Entered Harvard University in 1884, and graduated with the degree A. B. in 1888. Since graduation has been engaged in journalism, writing for most of the Boston dailies Member of Knights of Columbus, South Boston Historical Society, A. O. H., Catholic Alumni club of Boston, and other societies. On special committee to prepare history of the "Ancient Codfish" that hangs in the hall of the House, and prepared the historical report of that committee. Committee on banks and banking in House of 1895; on committees on ways and means, and congressional redistricting in Boston in House of 1896; on committees on engrossed bills, mercantile affairs, and clerk of ways and means in Senate of 1897. On committees on ways and means rules, mercantile affairs, 1898.

Vote of district: A. Cummings, Republican, 1912; James A. Gallivan, Democrat, 5215.

Seventh District.—*Wards 16, 20, 24 of Boston.*—HON. CHARLES E. FOLSOM, Republican, was born in Boston, Feb. 24, 1855; educated in the public schools. In the paint and oil business. Member of the Boston common council in 1891 2; of the Boston board of aldermen in 1893-4 5 6. Appointed chief assessor by Mayor Quincy, May, 1898. Member of Dorchester council of Royal Arcanum, of the A. O. U. W., of the Home Circle and of the Old Dorchester club. Chairman of committee on public health; and on cities, and manufactures, in Senate of 1897. On committees on public health (chairman), cities, manufactures, 1898.

Vote of district: Charles E. Folsom, Republican, 5356; J. H. Griffin, Democrat, 2600.

Eighth District.—Wards 21, 22, 23 of Boston.—HON. WILLIAM W. DAVIS, Republican, was born in Cambridge, Aug. 6, 1862; educated in its public schools. In hotel business since 1888, and is manager of the Norfolk House, Boston. A. F. & A. M., Royal Arcanum, Home Circle, Mass. Hotel Association, H. M. M. B. A., Middlesex club, Dudley association, Lincoln Republican club. In Boston common council, 1894. Committee on insurance in House of 1895; clerk of committees on insurance and on State House, redistricting committee congressional recess committee investigating caucuses in city of Boston 1896; chairman of committee on election laws, and on libraries, and mercantile affairs, 1897. On committees on election laws (chairman), libraries (chairman), fisheries and game, mercantile affairs, 1898.

Vote of district: B. H. Couig, Democrat, 2768; William W. Davis, Republican, 5040.

Ninth District.—Wards 11, 19, 25 of Boston.—HON. JOSHUA BENNETT HOLDEN, of Boston, Republican, was born in Woburn, March 5, 1850; educated in private schools and Harvard Law School, class of 1871. Has charge of real estate in Boston and Lowell belonging to the Joshua Bennett estate and the estate of George Holden, and has also large real estate interests of his own to look after. Is a Knight Templar and 32d degree Mason; member of Algonquin club. Member of Boston common council, 1893-4. Has a fine country place at Billerica, which was the homestead of his parents and grandparents, and takes a great interest in the affairs of the town. Trustee of Bennett library of that town. Committee on railroads in House of 1895. On committees on constitutional amendments, and on railroads, 1896; also on special committee on redistricting the state. Chairman of committee on State House, and on federal relations, and railroads in Senate of 1897. On committees on State House (chairman), rules, railroads, 1898.

Vote of district: Joshua B. Holden, Republican, 4017; J. J. Porter, Democrat, 3202.

WORCESTER COUNTY.

First District.—Wards 4, 5, 6, 7, 8 of Worcester.—HON. ELLERY BICKNELL CRANE, Republican, of Worcester, was born in Colebrook, Coos county, N. H., Nov. 12, 1836. In 1837, with a few other families, his parents removed to the West and founded what is now the city of Beloit, Rock county, Wisconsin. Was here educated in the public schools and Beloit Seminary, the latter institution being the foundation of the present Beloit College. In April, 1867, removed to Worcester and has since lived there, being engaged in the lumber business. President of the Builders' Exchange, 1886-7-8. President of the Worcester county mechanics' association 1890-1891. President of the Worcester Society of Antiquity 1881 to 1893. In common council, 1876-7-8-9; in aldermen, 1886, and 1887; is also a director and a vice president of the Equity co-operative bank. Cast his first presidential vote for Abraham Lincoln, at a place called Strawberry Valley, situated on the Sierra Nevada Mountains, California, 1860. On committee on constitutional amendments in House of 1895; on elections, 1896. Chairman of committee on taxation, and on election laws, and roads and bridges in Senate of 1897. On committees on parishes and religious societies (chairman), roads and bridges, street railways, taxation, 1898.

Vote of district: Ellery B. Crane, Republican, 3386; E. J. McMahon, Democrat, 2178.

Second District.—Berlin, Bolton, Boylston, Clinton, Harvard, Holden, Lancaster, Sterling, West Boylston, Wards 1, 2, 3 of Worcester.—HON. ALFRED SEELYE ROE of Worcester, Republican, was born in Rose, Wayne county, N. Y., June 8, 1844. Graduated from Wesleyan University, 1870; from that date to

1875, principal of the Ashland, Mass., High school; from 1875 to 1880, a master in Worcester High school; and from 1880 to 1890 was principal of same. Served during the Rebellion in 9th New York Heavy Artillery, and was captured at Monocacy, Md., July 9, 1864, being held a prisoner till 22d of the following February. House chairman of committee on libraries, and on committee on education, 1892. House chairman of committee on education in House of 1893. Held same position in 1894; also clerk of committees on woman suffrage, and on committee on libraries; House chairman on education, clerk of committee on woman suffrage, and on committee on cities, 1895; on committees on education, (chairman); cities and State House. Senate of 1896; chairman of committee on education; and on cities, public service and State House, 1897. On committees on education (chairman), cities, State House, 1898.

Vote of district: J. F. McGovern, Democrat, 2015; Alfred S. Roe, Republican, 3817.

Third District:—Ashburnham, Athol, Fitchburg, Gardner, Leominster, Royalston, Westminster, Winchendon, Lunenburg—HON. HARDING R. BARBER of Athol, Republican, was born in Warwick, Dec. 20, 1839; educated in its public schools. Served as clerk in stores in Erving, Athol, Orange, Greenfield and South Royalston until 1862. Enlisted in Co. E, 53d Massachusetts infantry, August, 1862; discharged Sept. 2, 1863. Served three terms as worshipful master of Star lodge of Masons; Eastern Star lodge, Knights of Honor. Been in business of trunks, bags, harness and horse furnishing for nearly thirty years. Member of H. V. Smith post G. A. R. Committee on federal relations in House of 1895; committee on prisons, 1896. Chairman of committee on agriculture; and on parishes and religious societies, and prisons, 1897. On committees on agriculture (chairman), liquor law, prisons, towns, 1898.

Vote of district: Harding R. Barber, Republican, 5004; C. M. Day, Democrat, 1539.

Fourth District.—Barre, Brookfield, Charlton, Dana, Dudley, Hardwick, Hubbardston, Leicester, New Braintree, North Brookfield, Oakham, Paxton, Petersham, Phillipston, Princeton, Rutland, Southbridge, Spencer, Sturbridge, Templeton, Warren, Webster, West Brookfield.—HON. WILLIAM H. FAIRBANK of Warren, Republican, was born in Warren, April 3, 1836; educated in the public schools. General superintendent and engineer of telegraph and telephone lines. Began as contractor and builder at the age of nineteen, and has since been connected with almost every telegraph and telephone company in the country, building lines in nearly every state and city. President and life trustee of the Warren public library; vice president of Quaboag Historical Society; member of Quaboag lodge of Masons, and the Arcturus lodge of Odd Fellows. On committee on mercantile affairs, and on special committee on redistricting the state, 1896; on railroads in House of 1897; on committees on engrossed bills (chairman) federal relations, public charitable institutions, water supply, 1898.

Vote of district: H. C. Beaman, Democrat National, 385; Wilson H. Fairbank, Republican, 3543; R. J. Stevenson, Democrat, 1451.

Fifth District.—Auburn, Blackstone, Douglas, Grafton, Hopedale, Mendon, Milford, Millbury, Northborough, Northbridge, Oxford, Shrewsbury, Southborough, Sutton, Upton, Uxbridge, Westborough—HON WILLIAM H. COOK of Milford, Republican, born in Bennington, Vt., Jan. 7, 1843; educated in the public schools. Came to Massachusetts in 1872. Publisher of Milford Daily Journal and other papers. In House of 1877, committee on printing; in 1878, committee on Hoosac Tunnel. Was first president of Suburban Press Association, for three years; president of Mass. Press Association, two years; president of Massachusetts Republican Editorial Association, since it was established in 1891. Member of Stark lodge of Masons, Bennington, Vt. Chairman of committee on prisons and on liquor law, and engrossed bills; and on special committee on redistricting the State in Senate of 1896. Chairman of committees on liquor law, and prisons; and on committees on engrossed bills, and parishes and religious societies in Senate of 1897. On committees on liquor law (chairman), prisons (chairman), towns, 1898.

Vote of district: William H. Cook, Republican, 3418; G. H. Stoldard, Democrat, 1838.

COMPOSITE DISTRICTS

Berkshire and Hampshire.—*Alford, Becket, Egremont, Great Barrington, Lee, Lenox, Monterey, Mount Washington, New Marlboro, Otis, Richmond, Sandisfield, Sheffield, Stockbridge, Tyringham, Washington, West Stockbridge in Berkshire County; Chesterfield, Cummington Easthampton, Goshen, Hadley, Hatfield, Huntington, Middlefield, Northampton, Plainfield, South Hadley, Southampton, Westhampton, Williamsburg, Worthington in Hampshire county; Blandford, Chester, Russell in Hampden county*—HON. RICHARD W. IRWIN, of Northampton, Republican, was born in that city, Feb. 18, 1857; educated in public schools and Boston University Law School, class of 1885. After leaving public schools, learned machinist's trade in Florence Sewing Machine Company's shop. Then worked two and half years in machine department of Elgin (Ill.) Watch Company. Returned to Natick, and was in house-furnishing business with his brother, T. L. Irwin. Entered Boston University Law School in 1882, graduating with L L. B. in 1885. Admitted to Hampshire county bar same year, and has practiced in Northampton ever since. Member of common council, 1888 and 1889, president of same latter year. Now serving sixth consecutive year as city solicitor. First lieut. Co. I 2d regiment, from Nov. 25, 1887, to Aug. 27, 1889; capt. of same from latter date to Aug. 20, 1892, when resigned. Member of Nonotock lodge of Odd Fellows. Member of the local lodge of Masons. Clerk of committee on probate and insolvency, and on committee on constitutional amendments in the House of 1894; House chairman of committee on bills in 3d reading, on committees on judiciary and rules, and on the special committee to prepare a history of "Ye Ancient Codfish" in the hall of the House, 1895; chairman of committees on cities, and bills in third reading; and on counties, and on state redistricting committee. Senate of 1896; chairman of committee on street railways, and on judiciary, and rules, 1897. On committees on constitutional amendments (chairman), street railways (chairman), judiciary, 1898.

Vote of district: F. K. Hinckley, Democrat, 2442; Richard W. Irwin, Republican, 4994.

Berkshire District.—*Adams, Cheshire, Clarksburg, Dalton, Florida, Hancock, Hinsdale, Lanesboro, New Ashford, North Adams, Peru, Pittsfield, Savoy, Williamstown, Windsor.*—Hon. WILLIAM A. WHITTLESEY, Republican, was born in Danbury, Conn., February 21, 1849; educated in public schools of Danbury, and at Marietta College, Marietta, Ohio, class of 1870. In the wholesale woolen business in Detroit, Mich. for four years, and then in charge of the literary department of the Henry A. Tilden Company of New Lebanon, N. Y., for three years. Seven years in the lumber business in Wisconsin In 1887 took charge of the Pittsfield Illuminating Company, Pittsfield, Mass., which consolidated in two years with the Electric Company, of which he became treasurer and manager. For three years treasurer of the Stanley Electric Mfg. Company, established largely by his influence, and is now one of its directors. A director of the Agricultural national bank; president of the board of trade. A 32° Mason; member of Berkshire commandery of Knights Templar. Clerk of committee on roads and bridges, and on committee on State House in House of 1897; on committees on banks and banking (chairman), ways and means, water supply, 1898.

Vote of district: A. Town, Prohibition, 247; J. F. Van Deusen, Democrat, 2902; William A Whittlesey, Republican 4669.

Cape District.—Barnstable, Brewster, Bourne, Chatham, Dennis, Eastham, Falmouth, Harwich, Mashpee, Orleans, Provincetown, Sandwich, Truro, Wellfleet, and Yarmouth in the county of Barnstable; Chilmark, Cottage City, Edgartown, Gay Head, Gosnold, Tisbury, West Tisbury, in the county of Dukes; and Nantucket.—HON. WILLIAM A. MORSE, of Tisbury, Republican, born in Boston, July 27, 1863, but has always resided at Vineyard Haven, Martha's Vineyard. After completing his studies at the island schools, he studied at Hebron Academy, Me., and at Worcester Academy. Studied law with Knowlton & Perry, New Bedford, Prince & Peabody, Boston, and at Boston University. Admitted to Suffolk bar, Jan. 26, 1886, and since admitted to the United States circuit and district courts, and the United States supreme court. Is a lawyer, with offices in the Equitable Building, Boston. For the heroic rescue, by a perilous dive, of a fisherman's son from drowning at No Man's Island while he was still a law student, was given a valuable medal by the Massachusetts Humane Society. Member of Paul Revere lodge of Odd Fellows, Somerville; of Martha's Vineyard lodge of Masons. Also member of A. & A. Scottish Rite 32d degree, St. Andrews royal arch chapter, Aleppo Temple, Mystic Shrine. Ancient and Honorable Artillery Co., Boston lodge of Elks, Boston Press Club, and various clubs on Cape Cod and Martha's Vineyard. In House of Representatives, 1893, on committees on county estimates and State House. In Senate of 1895, chairman of committee on engrossed bills; and on committees on judiciary, and harbors and public lands. Chairman of committee on insurance; and on judiciary, and harbors and public lands, 1896. Chairman of committee on judiciary, and on counties, and harbors and public lands 1897. On committees on judiciary (chairman), fisheries and game, harbors and public lands, 1898.

Vote of district: H. L. Chipman, Prohibition, 261; William A. Morse, Republican, 2514; C. C. Paine, Democrat, 493.

Franklin-Hampshire District.—Amherst, Ashfield, Belchertown, Bernardston, Buckland, Charlemont, Colrain, Conway, Deerfield, Enfield, Erving, Gill, Granby, Greenfield, Greenwich, Hawley, Heath, Leverett, Leyden, Monroe, Montague, New Salem, Northfield, Orange, Pelham, Prescott, Rowe, Shelburne, Shutesbury, Sunderland, Ware, Warwick, Wendell, Whately.—HON. JOSEPH B. FARLEY, Republican, of Erving, was born in Colrain, Oct. 10, 1847; educated in the public schools and Shelburne Falls Academy. Began business as a merchant. Is now a paper manufacturer, being senior member of the well known Farley Paper Co. of Farley, which village, with his brother D. E., he founded in 1884. Is president of the Leavitt machine company of Orange, also interested in several other enterprises. Trustee of Orange savings bank and Orange co-operative bank. Was for some years lieutenant of Co. E, 2d Regiment M. V. M. Selectman of Orange in 1891-2, water commissioner 1893-4-5. Past master of lodge of the Temple and past high priest of Abanaque chapter of Masons. Is a Knight Templar; also an Odd Fellow, being a past grand, past high priest and past commandant. Member of the House in 1893-4, on committees on prisons (chairman in 1894,) and county estimates; Senate of 1897, chairman of committee on public service, and on ways and means, and street railways; on committees on ways and means (chairman), bills in 3d reading, public service, 1898.

Vote of district: Joseph B. Farley, Republican, 3725, S. Rockwell, Democrat, 1604.

THE CHAPLAIN AND CLERKS.

REV. EDMUND DOWSE, the chaplain, was born in Sherborn, Mass., September 17, 1813; graduated at Amherst College in 1836; was ordained and installed pastor of Pilgrim church, Sherborn, his native town, in 1838, and is still the only acting pastor. Was a member of the Massachusetts Senate in 1869 and 1870; was chosen chaplain of the Senate in 1880, and has been re-elected each succeeding year up to the present time.

HENRY DINGLEY COOLIDGE, of Concord, the clerk, was born in Chelsea, Aug. 26, 1858; was educated in the public schools; spent several years in mercantile business. Upon the death of the venerable Hon. Stephen N. Gifford, clerk of the Senate, in May, 1886, and the election of his assistant, E. H Clapp, as his successor, Mr. Coolidge was appointed by the latter as his assistant. He held this position in 1887 and 1888, and was unanimoulsy elected clerk in 1889, Mr. Clapp having removed from the state. He has been unanimously re-elected each year since.

WILLIAM H. SANGER, assistant clerk, was born in Louisville, Ky. March 12, 1862, his parents removing to Boston in 1866; attended the public schools of Boston and Hyde Park, graduating from the High school of the latter in 1880. After graduation did "suburban" work for the Boston Journal until 1889, when he was appointed to his present position. Resigning his connection with the Journal in 1888, took charge of the New England correspondence of the New York Sun, and held that position until 1894. Is now New England correspondent of the Philadelphia Inquirer.

KARL T. TAYLOR, clerical assistant, was born in Manchester, N. H., March 15, 1874; educated in the High school, Boston University College of Liberal Arts class of 1895, and Boston University Law School, class of 1898. Has been reporter on the Boston Journal and City Press Association. Clerical assistant in Senate, 1897 and 1898.

THE HOUSE OF REPRESENTATIVES.

THE SPEAKER.

HON. JOHN L. BATES, Republican, was born in (North) Easton, Sept. 18, 1859; educated in Boston public schools; Boston University, class of 1882; Boston University Law School, class of 1885. Taught school in Western New York, 1882-83, and in Boston in 1883-4; admitted to Suffolk bar, 1885, and practiced in Boston since that time. Member of common council, 1891-92. Trustee of Boston University. Director of Columbia trust company. President, 1893-4, of East Boston citizens' trade association; trustee of Meridian Street Methodist Bethel church and of Bromfield Street M. E. church. Member of Baalbec lodge of Masons, and of St. John's chapter: of Zenith lodge of Odd Fellows; of Royal Arcanum, and of A. O. U. W.; and president of the United Order of the Pilgrim Fathers, 1892-3 4. On committees on insurance and revision of corporation laws in House of 1894; House chairman of committee on insurance, and on committee on metropolitan affairs, 1895; chairman of House committee on bills in 3d reading, and on metropolitan affairs, 1896. Chosen Speaker of the House by unanimous votes in 1897 and 1898.

BARNSTABLE COUNTY.

District No. 1.—Barnstable, Bourne, Falmouth, Mashpee, Sandwich.—
SEBA A. HOLTON of Falmouth, Republican, was born in Erving, Aug. 30, 1847; educated in Powers Institute of Bernardston, and is an honorary graduate of Dartmouth College. For 10 years was principal of Lawrence Academy, Falmouth, and has since then been engaged in mercantile pursuits. On school com-

mittee in 1886-7. Chairman of Republican town committee 1884-95. Member of Marine lodge of Masons. On committee on education in House of 1896; on committee on taxation, 1898
Vote of district: Seba A. Holton, Republican. 876; W. D. Woodward, Prohibition, 67.

District No 2.—Chatham, Dennis, Harwich, Yarmouth.—LUTHER HALL, Republican, of Dennis was born in that town, Nov. 5, 1842; educated in the public schools. Was in the dry goods and grocery business, for 20 years; since that time has been in the commission business and in cranberry culture on an extended scale. Postmaster at Dennis from 1872 to 1884. Member of the school board since 1868, serving as chairman for the last 16 years and superintendent from 1880 to '91. A trustee in Bass River savings bank. Member of Hotel Men's mutual association; of Cape Cod lodge of Knights of Honor; and of the Royal Arcanum. Enlisted, Sept. 16, 1862, in the 5th regiment, and served nine months in the Department of North Carolina, term expiring, July 1, 1863; re-enlisted in same regiment, July 27, 1864, serving 100 days in the Eighth army corps; afterwards commissioned by Gov. Andrew as captain in the militia. Member of F. D. Hammond post No. 141. G. A. R. On committees on elections, and parishes and religious societies, 1897; on elections, and harbors and public lands, 1898.
Vote of district: J. H. Drum, Democrat, 119; Luther Hall, Republican, 680.

District No 3.—Brewster, Eastham, Orleans, Provincetown, Truro, Wellfleet.—THOMAS D. SEARS of Brewster, Republican, was born in that town, Feb. 22, 1845; educated in its public schools. Been a merchant for the last 25 years. Selectman 1878-86, inclusive; school committee for last eight years. Member of Exchange lodge of Odd Fellows. On committee on fisheries and game, 1898.
Vote of district: Thomas D. Sears, Republican, 597; all others, 1.

BERKSHIRE COUNTY.

District No. 1.—Clarksburg, North Adams.—JOHN EDWARD MAGENIS, Republican, of North Adams, was born there, May 5, 1873; educated in Drury Academy in North Adams; entered Boston University School of Law in 1891 and graduated as alternate class orator of the class of 1894. Admitted to the Berkshire bar in the same year and has since practiced law in North Adams. Especially prominent in the successful effort to modify the law of newspaper libel in 1897. On committee on judiciary in House of 1897; on the same, 1898.

FRANK STONE RICHARDSON of North Adams, Republican, was born in that city, Oct. 18, 1856; educated in its public schools. Treasurer and manager of the North Adams gas light company since 1878, and has also held the same offices with the Zylonite manufacturing company from 1887 to 1891. Treasurer of the North Adams fire district 1883-91. His record in the state militia is as follows: Enlisted as private in Co. C, 2d battalion infantry Feb. 8, 1878; served as 2d and 1st lieutenant and captain of Co. F, 2d regiment of infantry; colonel and assistant quartermaster general on the Governor's staff 1894-5-6; assistant inspector general 1st brigade M. V. M. at present. Clerk of committee on military affairs, and on committee on taxation, 1898.
Vote of district: John E. Magenis, Republican, 1362; J. P. Reed, Democrat, 790; Frank S. Richardson, Republican, 1399; J. J. Schreiber, Democrat, 410.

District No. 2.—Dalton, Hancock, Lanesborough, New Ashford, Williamstown.—ALMON E. HALL, Republican, of Williamstown, was born in Stamford, Vt., Dec. 6, 1846; educated in the public schools, Wesleyan Academy and Wesleyan University, class of 1872; and in the Boston University School of Theology.

Was a Methodist Episcopal minister until his health failed in 1877, and he was an invalid for 10 years. Since then has been engaged in farming, general merchandise and real estate business. Superintendent of schools in Stamford, Vt, 1880-1-2; chairman of Williamstown school committee in 1896-7-8. Clerk of committee on education, and on liquor law in House of 1897; on ways and means, and liquor law, 1898

Vote of district: Almon E. Hall, Republican, 645: W. C. Brague, Democrat, 65.

District No. 3.—*Adams, Cheshire, Florida, Savoy, Windsor*—JULIUS C. ANTHONY, Republican, of Adams, was born in that town, Sept. 24. 1856; educated in the public schools. Is a merchant. Member of Masons and of Knights Templar, being past master and past high priest; connected with fire department for 20 years. On committee on street railways in House of 1897; on street railways (clerk), 1898.

Vote of district: Julius C. Anthony, Republican, 690: J. M Morin, Democrat, 621.

District No 4.—*Pittsfield.*—DANIEL ENGLAND of Pittsfield, Democrat, was born in that city, July 1, 1868; educated in the public schools. Is a merchant, entering the dry goods firm of England Brothers in 1892. Member of the common council in 1897, on financial and fire department committees; member of the veteran firemen's association. Member of Mystic lodge of Masons. On committee on railroads, 1898.

JOHN M. STEVENSON of Pittsfield, Republican, was born in Cambridge, N. Y., Aug. 31, 1846; educated in public schools. Philips Academy at Andover, class of 1865; and two years at Yale College, class of 1869. Is in the insurance business, being the secretary and treasurer of the Berkshire Mutual fire insurance company since 1879. On committees on public charitable institutions, and pay roll, House of 1897; on fisheries and game, and public charitable institutions, 1898.

Vote of district: Daniel England, Democrat, 1580, G. W. Foot, prohibition, 38: J. W. Gamwell, Democrat, 1489; R. B Johnston, Republican. 1466: John M. Stevenson, Republican, 1490: A. B. Whipple, Prohibition, 29

District No. 5.—*Becket, Hinsdale, Lenox, Peru, Richmond, Washington. West Stockbridge.*—LUKE J. MACKEN, Democrat, of Hinsdale, was born in that town, Oct. 27, 1867; educated in the public schools, and in Eastman's Business College of Poughkeepsie, N. Y. Has been a commercial traveler for New York manufacturing chemists; postmaster for the last four years of the Cleveland administration. Member of Father Mathew total abstinence benevolent society and delegate to national convention in Scranton, Pa., 1897; member of Division 11 A. O. H. Clerk of committee on counties, 1898.

Vote of district: C. E. Lyman, Prohibition, 17; Luke J Macken. Democrat, 472: E. Tremain, Republican, 432.

District No. 6.—*Lee, New Marlborough, Otis. Sandisfield, Stockbridge, Tyringham.*—WILLIAM A. NETTLETON. Republican, of Stockbridge, was born Aug. 11, 1832, in Goshen, Ct.; educated in Williams Academy and Williams College, class of 1855 Has been engaged in mercantile, manufacturing and farming business. On committees on constitutional amendments, and education, 1898.

Vote of district: D. B. Finn, Democrat, 375; William A. Nettleton, Republican, 595.

District No. 7.—*Alford, Egremont, Great Barrington, Monterey, Mt. Washington, Sheffield.*—GEORGE W. MELLEN, sound money Democrat, Great Barrington, born in Hartford, Ct., May, 11, 1837; public schools Boot and shoe business. Selectman 1890-1-2-3. Masons. Committee on towns, House of 1897-8.

Vote of district: F. H. Briggs, Republican, 557; G. W. Mellen, Democrat, 786.

BRISTOL COUNTY.

District No. 1.—Attleboro, North Attleboro, Norton, Rehoboth, Seekonk.— ALFRED R. CROSBY, Republican, of Attleboro, was born in Glover, Vt., Aug. 30, 1838; educated in public schools and academy. Since 1874 has been member of the firm of Smith & Crosby, manufacturing jewelers. Enlisted Sept. 26, 1861, in Co. M, 1st New Hampshire artillery, and served in the Army of the Potomac. Mustered out in June 1865. Member of Wm. A. Streeter post No. 145 G. A. R. Member of school board, 1887-93. Past master of E. Bates lodge of Masons; past high priest of King Hiram chapter; past thrice illustrious master of Attleboro council, and past eminent commander of Bristol commandery of Knights Templar. On committees on elections, and constitutional amendments in House of 1897; on same committees, 1898.

BURRILL PORTER, Jr., Republican of No. Attleboro, was born in Charlestown, N. H., Feb. 22, 1832. Educated in public schools of Langdon, N. H., in academies at Westminster and Saxton's River, Vt.; Dartmouth College, class of 1856. Was a teacher until 1879, during which time he taught academies in Canaan, Alstead, and Swanzey, N. H., and public schools in Cleveland and Fostoria, Ohio, and Braintree and Attleboro, Mass. Served five years as selectman, assessor and overseer of the poor, and collector of taxes of Attleboro; postmaster of North Attleboro four years, until July 1888. Represented First Bristol representative district in the Legislature of Massachusetts in 1881. Editor of the Evening Chronicle, North Attleboro. Member of Aurora lodge, No. 107, I. O. O. F. On committee on printing, and clerk of committee on constitutional amendments in House, 1893; House chairman of printing, and on towns, 1894; House chairman of printing and on education, 1895; House chairman of printing, and clerk of education, 1896; House chairman of education, 1897; House chairman of education, and on towns, 1898.

Vote of district: Alfred R. Crosby, Republican, 938; Burrill Porter, Jr., Republican, 879; all others none.

*District No. 2.—Easton, Mansfield, Raynham.—*FRANK W. BARNARD, Republican, of Mansfield, was born in Wrentham, Jan. 3, 1853; educated in the public schools and Day's academy. Was in the jewelry business; now in real estate and insurance. Chairman of Republican town committee for three years; member of board of registrars four years; tax collector one year. Past master of St. James lodge of Masons. On committee on labor in House of 1897; on committees on drainage and labor, 1898.

Vote of district: Frank W. Barnard, Republican, 540; H. W. Heath, Democrat, 331.

*District No. 3.—Wards 5, 7, 8, Taunton.—*EUGENE E. DONOVAN, Democrat, of Taunton, was born in Andover, Nov. 21, 1858; educated in the public schools. Is a dyer. Member of Sabbatia council No. 1345 of Royal Arcanum, of Catholic Benevolent Legion and of Whittenton Catholic Temperance Society. On committee on election laws, 1898.

Vote of district: Eugene E. Donovan, Democrat, 609; L. Mason, Republican, 607.

*District No. 4.—Wards 2, 3, 4 of Taunton.—*SILAS D. REED, Republican, was born there, June 25, 1872; educated in the public schools, and Bristol Academy, class of 1889; Amherst College, class of 1893; Boston University Law School during years 1894 and 1895. Since summer of 1895 in law office with

Ex-Mayor Charles A. Reed of Taunton. Prominent and active locally in secret fraternities; thirty-second degree Mason and a Shriner; past grand of Sabbatia lodge of Odd Fellows, also member of Naomi encampment and Canton Cohannet; member of Taunton past grands' association; past chancellor Taunton lodge K. of P.; first past officer El Kalif Temple, Knights of Khorassan, the original Knights of Khorassan in the New England states; member of grand lodge Knights of Pythias; member of Eastern past chancellors' association; member of League of American Wheelmen, the Taunton Cycle Club and the Bristol county wheelmen; member of Massachusetts Republican club, and Taunton Republican club. Life member of Old Colony Historical Society and Bristol County agricultural society. Member of Republican city committee in 1898. Fraternity editor of Taunton Evening News, 1896; on committee on railroads in the House of 1897; clerk of same committee, 1898.

Vote of district: Silas D. Reed, Republican, 691; all others, 4.

*District No. 5.—Berkley, Dighton, Wards 1, 6 of Taunton.—*JOSEPH M. PHILBRICK of Taunton, Republican, was born in that city, Nov. 20, 1869, and was educated in its public schools and Bryant & Stratton's Commercial College of Boston. Was a book-keeper for three years, but for the past four years has been a travelling salesman. Member of common council 1893, and of board of aldermen 1894-5. Member of Sabbatia lodge of Odd Fellows. On committees on federal relations and water supply, 1898.

Vote of district: Joseph M. Philbrick, Republican, 604; all others, none.

*District No. 6.—Acushnet, Dartmouth, Fair Haven, Freetown.—*JOHN O. SLOCUM of Dartmouth, Republican, born there March 13, 1842; Friends' school, Pierce Academy. Farmer. Town auditing committee; road commissioner. Masons. Clerk of fisheries and game, House of 1896; same committee, 1898.

Vote of district, W. H. Potter, Republican Independent N. P., 178; John O. Slocum, Republican, 421.

*District No. 7.—Wards 1, 2, 3 of New Bedford.—*THOMAS M. DENHAM, Republican, of New Bedford, born there Feb. 2, 1840; educated in public schools, graduating from the High school in 1856. Until 1860 was clerk and reporter for the Daily Standard and Daily Mercury. During the war employed in post-office department and engaged in wholesale sutlering business. Since 1868 has been carrying on the manufacture of fine shirts under the firm name of T. M. Denham & Brother, doing an extensive business. Common council 1876; Republican city committee since 1894, chairman 1896-7. House 1895, committee on prisons; chairman same committee 1896-7-8, also committee on election laws, 1898.

SAMUEL ROSS, Republican, of New Bedford, was born in Cheshire, Eng., Feb. 2, 1865; public schools. Is a cotton mule spinner. Has been prominent in labor circles, and was president of the National cotton mlue spinners' association at its inception and is now secretary of the same and of the New Bedford mule spinners' association. In the House of 1892, on committee on labor; House chairman of same in 1893-4-5-6-7-8; also in 1895-6 on State House; and in 1897 also on libraries.

Vote of district: H. W. Butler, Democrat, 356; Thomas M. Denham, Republican, 1043; E. M. Murphy, Democrat, 351; Samuel Ross, Republican, 1069.

*District No. 8.—Wards 4, 5, 6 of New Bedford.—*WILLIAM J. BULLOCK, Republican, of New Bedford, born in Fall River, Jan. 31, 1864; public schools. Pharmacist. Common council 1897. Member of K. of P.; Red Men. Clerk committee on public health, 1898.

FRANK W. FRANCIS, Republican, of New Bedford, born there Sept. 16,

1857: public schools. Cigar manufacturer and tobacconist. Masons, Odd Fellows, K. of P., A. O. U. W.; House of 1892, committee on State House, clerk of committee on county estimates; 1896, counties; 1897, harbors and public lands; 1898, chairman of same.
Vote of district: William J. Bullock, Republican, 1078; O. S. Cook, Democrat, 290; Frank W. Francis, Republican, 1151; C. J. McGurk, Democrat, 748.

District No. 9.—Wards 1, 2, of Fall River, Westport.—JOHN W. CONNELLY, Democrat, of Fall River, born in that city, July 16, 1874; public schools; Boston University Law School. Lawyer. Committee on mercantile affairs, 1898.

JAMES WHITEHEAD, Republican, of Fall River, born in Lancashire, England, Dec. 20, 1857. Common schools. Weaver. Secretary of the Weavers' progressive association; secretary of Court Progress F. O. A.; and also a P. C. R. Committee on labor in House of 1897; same, 1898.
Vote of district: J. W. Connelly, Democrat, 855; E. Handy, Democrat, 398; Robert Howard, Independent, 843; J. Preston, Republican, 761; James Whitehead, Republican, 1021.

District No. 10.—Wards 3, 4, 5 of Fall River.—THOMAS DONAHUE, Democrat, of Fall River, born in Dublin, Ire., Aug. 20, 1853; public schools. Asst. assessor, 1887-8; 1892-3-4. Foresters; A. O. H.; Young Irish American Society. Committee on woman suffrage House of 1895; liquor law, 1896; clerk labor, 1897; clerk of labor, and on prisons, 1898.

MICHAEL B. JONES, Democrat, of Fall River, was born in that city, Aug. 20, 1864; public schools. Common council 1887-8; registrar 1892-6; committee on counties, 1898.
Vote of district: Thomas Donahue, Democrat, 2049; T. Gamache, Republican, 694; Michael B. Jones, Democrat, 2029; W. Mitchell, Republican, 781.

District No. 11.—Wards 6, 7, 8, 9 of Fall River, Somerset, Swansea.—HUGO A. DUBUQUE, of Fall River, Republican, was born in Canada, Nov. 3, 1854; educated in the public schools and a Canadian college. Degree of LL. B. at Boston University Law School, 1876 7. Is a lawyer. Past chancellor of Lafayette lodge of Knights of Pythias. Member of House of 1889, on judiciary committee; in 1897 8 on same committee.

ALEXANDER LOCKHART, Republican, of Fall River, born in north of Ireland. Dec. 22, 1854; public schools. Overseer in cotton mill. Common council 1880; aldermen, 1891-2. Committee on taxation, House of 1897; street railways, 1898.

ANDREW H. MORRISON, Republican, of Fall River, was born in that city, June 27, 1871; educated in the public schools. Is in the dry goods business firm of David Morrison & Son. Member of Fall River common council in 1897. On committee on harbors and public lands in House of 1898.
Vote of district: T. J. Boyce, Democrat, 982; Hugo A. Dubuque, Republican, 2425; T. Evans, Citizens, 363; J. J. Highland, Democrat, 1333; Alexander Lockhart, Republican, 2380; W. Miller, Prohibition, 356; Andrew H. Morrison, Republican, 2180; P. E. Sullivan, Democrat, 925.

DUKES COUNTY.

District No. 1.—Chilmark, Cottage City, Edgartown, Gay Head, Gosnold. Tisbury, West Tisbury.—WILLIAM A. SWIFT of Tisbury, Prohibitionist, was born in that town (Vineyard Haven), Nov. 1, 1860; educated in the public schools. Has been a retail grocer for 13 years. Town clerk since March, 1885.

Clerk of committee on federal relations, and on parishes and religious societies, 1898.

Vote of district: Otis Foss, Republican, 277; William S. Swift, Prohibition, 327.

ESSEX COUNTY.

District No. 1.—Amesbury.—DANIEL W. DAVIS, Republican, born in Shapleigh, Me., Oct. 3, 1846; public schools, New Hampton Academy, class of 1882. Enlisted in June, 1863, not assigned to any regiment; enlisted July, 1864, in Co. I, 1st Maine cavalry; served in Army of the Potomac; severely injured before Petersburg; mustered out, Aug. 14, 1865. Member of E. P. Wallace post No. 122 G. A. R., chaplain. Is a shoemaker, teacher; member of school board, 1887-93. Postmaster at Amesbury, 1892-6. Member of Mt. Prospect lodge of Masons of Ashland, N. H.; Trinity chapter of Amesbury; of Mt. Pleasant lodge of Odd Fellows of Dover, N. H., and of the Ancient Order of United Workmen. Clerk of committee on parishes and religious societies, in House of 1897; House chairman of same committee, and clerk of printing, 1898.

Vote of district: Daniel W. Davis, Republican, 662; J. L. Tibbetts, Democrat, 215.

District No. 2.—Merrimac, Ward 6 of Newburyport, Salisbury, West Newbury.—BENJAMIN F. STANLEY of Newburyport, Republican, was born in North Berwick, Me., Nov. 6, 1823, and was educated in the public schools. Is a ship carpenter. Member of common council in 1869 and 1882-3-4, and of board of aldermen in 1885-6. Member of Quascacunquen lodge of Odd Fellows. On committee on roads and bridges, 1898.

Vote of district: A. Hoyt, Democrat, 199; J. F. Spaulding, Prohibition, 103; Benjamin F. Stanley, Republican, 511.

District No. 3.—Wards 4, 5, 6 of Haverhill.—CARLETON F. HOW, Republican, of Haverhill, was born in that city, April 20, 1863; educated in the public schools, with one year in the class of 1884, Harvard College. Was in the leather business, but since then has been in the life and accident insurance business. Member of the Haverhill school committee 1888-95, inclusive. Member of the Elks. Clerk of committee on banks and banking, 1898.

Vote of district: J. N. B. Green, Democrat, 357; Carleton F. How, Republican, 500; R. L. Wood, Republican Independent, N. P., 369.

District No. 4.—Wards 1, 2, 3 of Haverhill.—GEORGE H. CARLETON, Republican, of Haverhill, was born in that city, Aug 6, 1840, being a descendant in the ninth generation from Lieut. Edward Carleton, who was a member of the General Court in 1638; educated in the public schools, High school, class of 1857. Taught school until 1868, and was then in the shoe business for 25 years. Member of common council in 1871-2-3, being president the last two years. Mayor of Haverhill in 1888. President of the Pentucket savings bank since it was organized in 1891; vice president of Second national bank of Haverhill since its organization in 1886; president of the Haverhill Whittier club; trustee of Haverhill public library. On committee on ways and means in House of 1898.

Vote of district: George H. Carleton, Republican, 542; J. F. Dailey, Socialist Labor, 68; J. H. Nolan, Democrat, 427; E. Sherman, Democrat Independent N. P., 47.

District No. 5.—Ward 5, of Haverhill.—GEORGE H. BARTLETT, Republican, of Haverhill; born in Kingston, N. H., Sept. 6, 1857; public schools. Shoe manufacturer. Common council 1884-6. Masons. Director in Haverhill Co-operative bank. Committee on drainage; 1897, water supply; 1898, clerk of same, and chairman of pay roll.

Vote of district: George H. Bartlett, Republican, 401; M. T. Berry, Socialist Labor, 114; R. J. Davis, Democrat, 254.

District No. 6.—Wards 1, 2 of Lawrence, Methuen.—GEORGE G. FREDERICK, Republican, Methuen; born Jan. 14, 1867; public schools, Mass. College of Pharmacy. Druggist. Odd Fellows. K of P. Clerk of committee on manufactures House 1897-8.

GEORGE B. SMART, Republican, of Lawrence, born in Berwick, Me., Feb. 25, 1835; public schools Coppersmith, plumber Common council two years, board of health six years. K. of H. Committee on drainage, House of 1897; same and public health, 1898.

Vote of district: L. S. Crosby, Prohibition, 75; C. F. Drescner, Democrat, 1264; George G. Frederick, Republican, 1451; J. C. Sanborn, jr., Democrat, 1171; George B. Smart, Republican, 1341; W. F. Taylor, Prohibition, 63.

District No. 7.—Wards 3, 4, 5, 6 of Lawrence.—RICHARD CULLINANE, Democrat, of Lawrence, was born in Ireland, Feb. 2, 1859; removed to Lawrence, May 11, 1864; educated in public schools and Cannon's Commercial College and Comer's Commercial School. Is a carpenter. Was instructor in architectural, isometric and geometrical drawing and autographic projection in evening school for past three years, conducted under auspices of the Carpenters' Union. Prominent in labor matters for many years; member of Carpenters' Brotherhood; president of Union No. 111 six consecutive terms; instrumental in organizing Lawrence Central Labor Union in 1893; chairman of its building committee three consecutive terms; president of Central Labor Union in 1894-5-6-7; attended many conventions of American Federation of Labor. Member of Court Essex No. 90 Foresters of America; member of Samoset colony of Pilgrim Fathers. On committee on labor in House of 1897; on committees on labor, and State House, 1898.

JOSEPH H. JOUBERT, Democrat, of Lawrence, was born in Yellow Springs, O., April 6, 1860; educated in the public schools and in Ticonderoga, Academy of Ticonderoga, N. Y. Has been a weaver, loom fixer, and tobacconist. Assistant assessor 1890-7. Member of Miantonomoh colony of Pilgrim Fathers, and of Montgomery court of Foresters Captain of Co. F. 9th regiment of infantry and went at head of his company into camp at Camp Dewey, South Framingham, M'y 4, 1898, and subsequently went with his company to "Camp Alger", Va., Tuesday May 31. On committees on engrossed bills, and libraries, 1898.

CORNELIUS F. SULLIVAN, Democrat, of Lawrence, was born in that city June 15, 1865; public schools. Tea merchant. Common council, 1891: overseer of poor, 1892. Pilgrim Fathers; A. O. U. W. Committee on insurance, 1896; banks and banking, 1897; same, 1898.

Vote of district: B. C. Ames, Republican, 2005; J. Barker, Prohibition, 157; Richard Cullinane, Democrat. 2700; J. S. Curnew, Prohibition, 207; Joseph H Joubert, Democrat, 2667; E. F. Kennedy, Republican, 1815; M. Manahan, Republican, 1847; Cornelius F. Sullivan, Democrat, 2501.

District No. 8.—Andover, Middleton, North Andover.—ALBERT POOR, Republican, of Andover, born in North Andover; Harvard College, 1879; Harvard Law School, 1882. Lawyer. B. A. A., Boston Art Club, University club. Committee on railroads, 1898.

Vote of district: Albert Poor, Republican, 990; all others, 11.

District No. 9 —Boxford, Georgetown, Groveland, Ward 7 of Haverhill, (formerly Bradford.)—EDWARD H. HOYT, Republican, of Bradford, was born in Haverhill, July 11, 1849; educated at Phillips Exeter and Andover academies. Has been in leather business and electric railways, but has now retired. Member of Union lodge of Masons, of St. Paul's chapter, of Boston council, and of Boston commandery of Knights Templar, of Massachusetts consistory; past T. P. G. M. of Merrimack Valley Lodge of Perfection, past exalted ruler of Haverhill lodge of Elks; and past chancellor of Ingomar lodge of Knights of Pythias. On committee on street railways in House of 1897; chairman of same committee, 1898.

Vote of district: Edward H. Hoyt, Republican, 516; J. F. White, Democrat, 297.

District No. 10.—Danvers, Peabody, Topsfield.—ADDISON P. LEAROYD, Republican, of Danvers, was born in that town, Feb. 11, 1838; educated in the public schools. Member of the school committee from 1881 to date; member of the water board in 1889; town treasurer from 1890 to date. On committee on State House in 1898.

ABELARD E. WELLS of Peabody, Republican, was born in Portland, Me., June 17, 1854; educated at Westbrook Academy, class of 1875, and at Tufts College class of 1879. Principal of Bowditch school, Peabody, from 1879 to 1889; in 1890 traveled through New England in interest of Dodd, Mead & Co., New York publishers; from 1890 to the present has been in life insurance business. Selectman 1895-6, chairman the last year; on school committee for past four years and is at present the chairman. Member of Jordan lodge of Masons, of Washington royal arch chapter, and of Winslow Lewis commandery of Knights Templar. Member of Holten lodge of Odd Fellows; Peabody board of trade. On committee on election laws (clerk), and on printing, 1898.

Vote of district: N. A. Bushby, Democrat, 959; T. J. Gallivan, Democrat, 764; Addison P. Learoyd, Republican, 1279; Abelard E. Wells, Republican, 1092.

District No. 11.—Ward 3, of Lynn, Swampscott.—JAMES F. SEAVEY of Lynn, Republican, born in Greenland, N. H., Dec. 6, 1842; public schools, North Hampton (N. H.) Academy. Carpenter; contractor in Lynn 22 years. Common council 1893-4-5; aldermen 1895-6. Committee on street railways, 1898.

ROBERT S. SISSON of Lynn, Republican, was born in that city, June 4, 1846, and was educated in the public schools. Has been letter carrier, manager of the local branch of Singer Manufacturing Company, and later with L. A. May & Co., house furnishers, and now of Pitman, Newhall & Sisson, real estate and insurance. Member of common council 1888-9-90. Member of overseers of the poor and chairman of the board since 1892. Past grand of East Lynn lodge of Odd Fellows; director and treasurer of East Lynn Odd Fellows' building association; past grand councillor of Massachusetts order of United Friends. Clerk of committee on public charitable institutions, 1898.

Vote of district: W. B. Gould, Democrat National, 86; I. Graves, Democratic National, 130; E. Keay, Prohibition, 63; S. P. Kenyon, Democrat, 484; M. E. Nies, Democrat, 421; J. W. Osborne, Prohibition, 90; James F. Seavey, Republican, 1324; Robert S. Sisson, Republican, 1362.

District No. 12.—Wards 1, 5, 7 of Lynn, Lynfield.—CHARLES O. BEEDE, Republican, of Lynn, born in Lynn, Dec. 29, 1840; educated in public schools and New Hampton (N. H.) Institute, class of 1857. Shoe manufacturer, dealer in leather supplies, rubber business in Boston; real estate. Alderman in 1881-2; water board. Director of the Manufacturers' national bank, a trustee of Lynn safe deposit and trust company, also of Lynn Five Cent savings bank; board of trade. Member of Mount Carmel lodge, Sutton royal arch chapter, and Olivet commandery Knights Templar of Masons. Committees on roads and bridges, and parishes and religious societies, 1897; on committee on metropolitan affairs, 1898.

WILLIAM H. SEVERANCE, Republican, of Lynn, was born in Bangor, Me., Jan. 12, 1858; public schools. In provision business for a number of years, but is now in the express business. Member of the common council in 1893-4. Member of Glenmere lodge of Odd Fellows, of Peter Woodland lodge of Knights of Pythias, and of Winepurkit tribe of Red Men. Director of Lynn co-operative bank. On committee on drainage in House of 1897, and clerk of same committee in 1898.

Vote of district: G. E. Batchelder, Prohibition, 81; Charles O. Beede, Republican, 1066; F. F. French, Democrat National, 149; J. W. Healey, Democrat National, 103; W. S. Hoyt, Democrat, 450; W. H. Keay, Prohibition, 48; J E. Rich, Democrat, 613; William H. Severance, Republican, 935.

District No. 13 —Wards 4, 2 of Lynn, Nahant.—HENRY C. ATTWILL, of Lynn, Republican, was born in that city March 11, 1872; educated in the public schools and Boston University Law School class of 1893. Is a lawyer. Member of committee on probate and insolvency, and clerk of committee on elections (House,) 1896; clerk of House and joint judiciary, 1897; on judiciary committee, 1898.

CHARLES H. RAMSDELL of Lynn, Republican, was born in Lynn, Sept. 26, 1840, and was educated in its public schools. Enlisted July 11, 1864, in Co. D, 8th regiment and served in Baltimore; mustered out Nov. 10, 1864; member of Gen. Lander post 5, G. A. R. In the grocery and real estate business. Member of common council 1892-3-4, and of the aldermen 1895-6. Member of Glenmere lodge of Odd Fellows, treasurer 1885 to 1888; member of Palestine encampment; also of Winepurkit tribe of Red Men; engineer of fire department twelve years. On committees on parishes and religious societies, and public service, 1898.

Vote of district: Henry C. Attwill, Republican, 1200; G. A. Bettenhausen, Democrat, 448; S. A. Breed, Democratic National, 106; H. E Chase, Prohibition, 90; G. N Goodridge, Prohibition, 76; D. W. Goodwin, Democratic National, 98; L. R. Pierce, Democrat, 485; Charles H. Ramsdell, Republican, 1090.

District No 14 —Ward 6 of Lynn, Saugus.—FRANK P. BENNETT, Republican, of Saugus was born in Cambridge, May 2, 1853; educated in Malden and Chelsea public schools. Always been engaged in journalism, making a specialty of financial subjects. Proprietor and editor of "The Wool and Cotton Reporter" and owner of the "United States Investor." Served as auditor and selectman while residing in Everett, and was in House of 1891-2-3-4 from that town. House chairman of committee on taxation in 1891, and on special committee on administrative boards and commissions; in 1892, House chairman of rapid transit committee, on rules, and joint special committee on public reservations; in 1893, House chairman of special committees on rapid transit, and public reservations, and on rules; in 1894 declined all committee appointments, except on rules; in 1898, House chairman of committee on agriculture, and on election laws.

GEORGE F. HARWOOD, Republican, of Lynn, was born in Halifax, England, July 7, 1844, but removed to this country at an early age; educated in private schools of Danvers. In the crockery and glass ware business until 1893, and since then has been in the real estate business. Member of common council in 1893-4-5, and of the board of aldermen in 1896-7. Member of Pine Grove cemetery commissioners. Member of Providence lodge of Odd Fellows. On committee on cities, 1898.

Vote of district: Frank P. Bennett, Republican, 1244; L. M. Brock, Democrat, 871; G. R Brougham, Prohibition, 74; M. F. Cunningham, Democrat, 893; G. W. Foster, Democrat National, 77; D. C. Grover, Prohibition, 78; George F. Harwood, Republican, 1266.

District No. 15.—Marblehead.—WILLIAM BRIDGEO of Marblehead, Democrat, was born in that town, Oct. 14, 1850; educated in its public schools. Shoe manufacturer. Member of committee on federal relations, 1898.

Vote of district: A. P. Alley, Republican Independent N. P., 31; William Bridgeo, Democrat, 568; I. S. Freeto, Independent, 136; P. Howard Shirley, Republican, 430.

District No. 16 — Wards 1, 2 of Salem. — WILLIAM D. CHAPPLE, Republican, was born in that city Aug 6, 1868; educated in the public schools and Boston University Law School, class of 1890. Admitted to the bar in the same year and has practiced in Salem ever since. Member of Salem common council 1894-5-6, being president of the board in the last year. Member of Starr King lodge of Masons; Sutton Lodge of Perfection; past grand of Fraternity lodge of Odd Fellows. On Republican city committee for the last six years; president of the Young Men's Republican club of Salem. Member of committee on probate and insolvency, House of 1897; on special committee on the impeachment of Melville P. Morrill. House chairman of probate and insolvency, 1898.

Vote of district: William D. Chapple, Republican, 717; M. J. Daly, Democrat, 380.

District No. 17. — Wards 3, 5 of Salem. — J. FRANK DALTON of Salem, Republican, was born in that city, April 19, 1842, and was educated in its public schools. Enlisted in the United States Navy in 1861, serving until 1865 on "Katahdin" and "Oneida"; past commander of P. H. Sheridan post 34 G. A. R. Member of Second Corps of Cadets from 1865 to 1891, being its commander eight years. In the insurance and real estate business. Trustee of Salem Five Cents savings bank, and on board of managers of Bertram Home for Aged Men and Old Ladies' Home. Deputy collector of customs for Salem in 1878-81. Postmaster 1881-91. In common council 1873; board of aldermen 1893; overseer of the poor nine years; on the school committee three years. Member of Essex lodge of Masons. On committee on insurance, 1898.

Vote of district: J. Frank Dalton, Republican, 876; F. P. Keegan, Democrat, 282.

District No. 18. — Wards 4, 6 of Salem. — CHARLES E. TROW, Republican, born in Hamilton, April 18, 1833; educated in the public schools in that town, and at Thetford Academy. He became a teacher but later was engaged in mercantile pursuits, which he left to enter the field of journalism. Member of the Lawrence Daily American staff when Major George S. Merrill was editor and proprietor of that paper. Subsequently he purchased the Methuen Transcript, of which paper he was editor and owner for 10 years His connection with the newspaper press in Salem, as editor, is well known, and covers a period of eleven years. He was editor of the Evening Telegram for some time and has since been identified with other local publications. When connected with the Boston Traveler some years ago he wrote a series of interesting articles entitled "Salem Shipmasters," which were continued for a year or more and were widely read. Served in the late war, enlisting in Co. G, 42d regiment, Mass. Volunteers, which was subsequently known as the "7th unattached company" in which organization he was a non-commissioned officer. Veteran member of the Boston Fusileers. Past chaplain of Phil H. Sheridan post 34 G. A. R.; past commander of Col. William B. Green post; Dept. Commander's staff, G. A. R.; past regent of Salem council Royal Arcanum; Loyal Americans, and has been a member of the Masonic order for over 25 years. He has performed efficient work for the Republican party, both as a writer and speaker in the advocacy of its principles. On committee on education, 1897; on committee on railroads, 1898.

Vote of district: E. C. Cody, Democrat, 418; Charles E. Trow, Republican, 647.

District No 19 —Beverly, Essex, Ward 8 of Gloucester, Hamilton, Manchester, Wenham —SAMUEL COLE, Republican, of Beverly, was born, Dec. 15, 1856, in Rutland, Vt Educated in the public schools. Is a market gardener. Member of the school committee eleven years, 1882-94; two years, 1895-6, president of the common council. Member of board of directors of the savings and co-operative bank; president of board of trade. Treasurer of Liberty lodge of Masons; member of Amity chapter and St. George commandery. Member of Bass River lodge of Odd Fellows, of Roger Conant council of Royal Arcanum, and of the United Order of American Mechanics. On committee on cities in House of 1897; clerk of same committee, and on engrossed bills, 1898.

HARRY CHOATE FOSTER, Republican, of Gloucester, was born in Swampscott, Aug. 27, 1870, educated in public and private schools and Institute of Technology. Is a civil engineer. Member of Republican city committee in 1897-8. Member of Tyrian lodge of Masons On committee on roads and bridges in 1898.

Vote of district: Samuel Cole, Republican, 1364; F. A Foster, Democrat, 381; Harry C. Foster, Republican, 1154; F. E. Lee, Democrat, 290.

District No. 20.—Ward 1, 3, 4, 5, 6 of Gloucester. - JOHN FAVOR of Gloucester, Republican, was born in that city, March 1, 1859, and was educated in the public schools Is a telegrapher and electrical contractor. Member of common council 1885-86-88; of board of aldermen 1894-5. Member of Bethlehem commandery Knights Templar, and of Constantine lodge of Knights of Pythias; member of the Republican ward and city committee; treasurer and superintendent of the Gloucester district messenger company. On committee on water supply, 1898.

HARVEY C SMITH, Republican, of Gloucester, was born in Rockport, Nov. 20, 1847; educated in the public schools and Bryant & Stratton's Commercial College of Boston. Master of vessel, 1870-71; wholesale fish dealer since 1872. Member of the common council 1889-90; board of aldermen in 1892. Member of the Republican city committee 1889-1897; chairman of same in 1896. Past noble grand of Ocean lodge of Odd Fellows, past chief patriarch of Cape Ann encampment; charter member of Wingaersheek tribe of Red Men; member of the Society of Colonial Wars and of the Sons of the American Revolution; also of Master Mariners' association of Gloucester. On committee on fisheries and game in House of 1897; clerk of same committee, and on printing, 1898.

Vote of district: Elliott Adams, Republican People's N. P., 400; A. P. Babson, Republican Citizens N. P., 175; Henry A. Burnham, Republican Independent N. P., 558; A. N Donahoe. Independent Citizens, 217; John Favor, Republican, 638; H. G. Lane, Republican Citizens N. P., 113; H. G Martin, Republican Independent N. P., 253; Harvey C. Smith, Republican, 731; M. Stevens, Independent, 55.

District No. 21 —Wards 2. 7 of Gloucester, Rockport.—LEANDER M. HASKINS of Rockport, (Gold Democrat antecedents) was born in that town, June 20, 1842, and was educated in Phillips Academy of Andover, and Dartmouth College 1862. Was a commissary clerk in the field with the 19th Army Corps at Port Hudson, La. Clerk in the Navy Department, Washington, 1863-68. Manufacturer and wholesale dealer of fish products, oils, ice, 1868-91 and of isinglass, 1879 to date. Member of Boston commandery of Knights Templar; member of Sons of American Revolution and Society of Colonial Wars; Rockport street railway company; president Sandy Bay Pier company. Director of Faneuil Hall national bank On committee on railroads, 1898.

Vote of district: E. O. Cleaves, Republican Peoples, 171; J. B. Donahue, Democrat Independent N. P., 5; B. Emerson, Republican Citizen N. P., 274;

Leander M. Haskins, Independent, 356; J. S. Parsons, Non-partisan, 27; W. Parsons Republican Labor N. P., 325.

District No. 22.—Ipswich, Newbury, Wards 1, 2, 3, 4, 5 of Newburyport. Ready.—WARREN BOYNTON, Republican, of Ipswich, was born in that town, July 17, 1836; educated in the public schools. Enlisted Feb. 25, 1862, in Co. A, 1st battery Heavy Artillery, served in Fort Warren and other places, promoted to sergeant, mustered out Oct. 20, 1865, having re-enlisted Feb. 29, 1864. Member of Gen. James Appleton post 128 G. A. R., and served as senior vice commander for three years. After the war was in the express business for 10 years, but has been in the hack and livery business for the last 18 years. Now serving his second term as registrar of voters. Member of Agawam lodge of Odd Fellows since Nov. 1, 1869, and has held all the usual lodge offices; also of Massasoit lodge A. O. U. W. On committees on pay roll, and printing in House of 1898.

CHARLES P. MILLS, Republican, of Newburyport, was born Aug. 22, 1853, in Yellow Springs, Ohio, son of Judge William and Ann Eliza Marshall Mills; educated in public schools of birthplace, at Lookout Mountain Educational Institution on the top of Lookout Mountain, Tenn.; and at Amherst College, where he graduated in 1874. Taught school in McCollom Academy, Mount Vernon, N. H., 1874-6. Graduated from Andover Theological Seminary in 1879, where an extra year was spent in private work with Professor Edward A. Park. Ordained to the gospel ministry and installed as pastor of the North Congregational church in Newburyport, Sept. 23, 1880, where he continues in active service. This is his first political office. On committee on fisheries and game, House of 1897; House chairman of same committee, and on parishes and religious societies, 1898.

Vote of district: Warren Boynton, Republican, 979; G. H. W. Hayes, Democrat, 315; H. B. Little, Democrat National, 213; Charles P. Mills, Republican, 1042; G. Prescott, Democrat National, 57; A. Withington, Democrat 509.

FRANKLIN COUNTY.

District No. 1.—Ashfield, Buckland, Charlemont, Colrain, Conway, Hawley, Heath, Monroe, Rowe, Shelburne.—GEORGE E. BEMIS of Charlemont, Republican, was born in Rowe, Oct. 23, 1855, and was educated in the public schools and Powers Institute of Bernardston. Has been teacher in the public schools and is now a jeweler. Member of school board for three years, and trustee of public library since 1891. Member of House in 1890, clerk of committee on agriculture, and on leave of absence; clerk of committee on agriculture in House of 1898.

Vote of district: George E. Bemis, Republican, 688; all others, 11.

District No. 2.—Bernardston, Gill, Greenfield, Leyden.—HERBERT COLLINS PARSONS, Republican, of Greenfield, was born in Northfield, Jan 15, 1862; educated in public schools and private high school. His father, A. C. Parsons, of Northfield was a member of the House in 1861 and of Senate in 1865. Early interested in journalism and became president New England Amateur Press Association. Became associate editor of the Greenfield Gazette and Courier on Jan. 1, 1889, and has since filled that position. On Northfield school committee 1886-9, chairman the last year. Now a member of the Greenfield school committee. Has served as chairman of various political committees of the Republican party. Member of Republican lodge of Masons. Vice president Suburban Press Association. In House of 1896, member of committees on constitutional amendments, and railroads; chairman of former and member of latter, 1897, and special committee to consider the impeachment of Norfolk county commissioners; on ways and means (clerk), and rules (clerk), 1898.

Vote of district: Herbert C. Parsons Republican, 672; G. H. Wright, Democrat, 334.

District No. 3.—Deerfield, Leverett, Montague, Sunderland, Wendell, Whately.—BENJAMIN W. MAYO, Republican, of Montague, Turners Falls, was born in (North) Orange, April 17, 1836; educated in the district school and at academies; taught school in winters. In 1857 entered local store and postoffice remaining there until enlistment Oct. 3, 1861, in Co. I, 25th regiment, serving with it in 9th and 18th army corps until term of three years expired, and then remained with the army until close of war in June, 1865. In a store and post-office in Templeton until 1871, when established store and postoffice in Turners Falls, remaining there as postmaster until 1895, being a presidential appointee from 1874. Past commander post 162, G. A. R., and has held nearly all of its offices. Member of Turners Falls board of trade from its organization. Committees on federal relations, and military affairs in House of 1896; committees on military affairs, and State House, 1897; on military affairs, and roads and bridges, 1898.

Vote of district: Benjamin W. Mayo, Republican, 613; G. Starbuck, Democrat, 499.

District No. 4.—Erving, New Salem, Northfield, Orange, Shutesbury, Warwick.—MARCUS M. STEBBINS, Republican, of Erving, was born in New Salem, Dec. 29, 1840; educated in the public schools. Enlisted Oct. 18, 1861, in Co. K. 26th regiment and was sergeant from Oct., 1861, to July, 1865, when he was mustered out. Member of G. A. R.; of board of selectmen; town clerk. Is a merchant. On committee on towns in House of 1898.

Vote of district: E. W. Hodges, Democrat, 312; Marcus M. Stebbins, Republican, 684.

HAMPDEN COUNTY.

District No. 1.—Brimfield, Holland, Monson, Palmer, Wales.—THOMAS W. KENEFICK, Democrat, of Palmer was born in Leominster, Sept. 17, 1855; educated in public schools, and Harvard College class of 1877. Studied law in Harvard Law School and in office of Hon. Charles R. Train of Boston. Admitted to the bar in 1879; practiced in Palmer since then. Clerk of committee on probate and insolvency, and on railroads in House of 1896; also on special committee to investigate the building of the Norfolk county court-house; in 1897, clerk of committee on rules, and on ways and means; in 1898, on same committees.

Vote of district: Thomas W. Kenefick, Democrat, 939; R. V. Sawin, Republican, 670.

District No. 2.—Agawam, East Longmeadow, Granville, Hampden, Longmeadow, Ludlow, Southwick, Tolland, Wilbraham.—ARTHUR D. KING, Republican, of Ludlow, was born in that town May 13, 1843; educated in the public schools. Enlisted Sept. 20, 1861, in Co. I, 27th regiment, promoted to be corporal. Member of Wilcox post 16, G. A. R. Employed in the United States armory in Springfield, then in gold and silver mining Colorado, but lately in the farming and meat business. Assessor from 1886 until the present. On committee on agriculture in House of 1898.

Vote of district: J. Haviland, Democrat, 300; Arthur D. King, Republican, 537.

District No. 3.—Wards 1, 2, 8 of Springfield.—GEORGE F. FULLER, Republican, Springfield, born in East Medway, March 8, 1842; public schools. Enlisted Aug. 25, 1862, in 11th Mass. Battery of Light Artillery. Grain and elevator business in Chicago until 1874, and since in wholesale grain business in Springfield. Common council, 1894; aldermen, 1895; E. K. Wilcox post G. A. R., Springfield. trustee of Winthrop club. Sons of the American Revolution. Committee on roads and bridges, House of 1896; House chairman of committee on roads and bridges, and on federal relations, 1897; House chairman of committee on printing, and on railroads, and monitor, 1898.

WILLMORE B. STONE, Democrat, of Springfield, was born in East Longmeadow, June 24, 1853; educated in public schools, took Harvard College course of four years, philosophic course, under private tutors. Associate member of E. K. Wilcox post No. 16 G. A. R. Attorney at law. Committee on judiciary in House of 1896; on same committee, and on rules, 1897; on same committees, 1898.

Vote of district: George F. Fuller, Republican, 1197; T. F. Loorem, Democrat Citizens N. P., 370; W. J. McCann, Democrat, 862; Willmore B. Stone, Democrat, 1130; C. L. Young, Republican, 889.

District No. 4.—Wards 3, 4, 5 of Springfield.—HENRY H. BOSWORTH Republican, of Springfield, was born in that city March 16, 1868; educated in its public schools and Amherst College, class of 1889. Studied law in Springfield, and is a practicing lawyer. Secretary of Ward Five Republican club, 1892-3; Secretary of Springfield improvement association, 1894-5; and its president, 1896. Clerk of committee on taxation in House of 1897; House chairman of committee on counties, and on taxation in House of 1898.

ALBERT T. FOLSOM, Republican, was born in Freeport, Me., Nov. 9 1831; educated in the public and private schools. City clerk and treasurer of Springfield from 1862 to 1887; bank director 20 years; president of Second national bank seven years; treasurer and trustee of the Union relief association 20 years; treasurer and director of the Improved Dwellings association 10 years; trustee of the Winthrop club; public administrator. On committee on cities of the House of 1897; on same committee, 1898.

Vote of district: Henry H. Bosworth, Republican 1348; Albert T. Folsom, Republican. 1316; E. A. Hall, Democrat, 571; J. E. Shipman, Democrat, 587.

District No. 5.—Wards 6, 7 of Springfield.—CHARLES E. HOAG, Republican, of Springfield was born in Moultonborough, N. H., Sept. 18, 1849; educated in public schools and academy and normal school. Read law with the late Judge Hill, admitted to the bar at Boston in 1876. Student and lawyer; author of several books; editor and proprietor of a newspaper eight years. Trustee of Peabody Institute six years. Member of Hampden lodge of Masons; Hampden lodge of Odd Fellows; Essex historical society; John G. Holland Senate of Ancient Essenic Order; American Mechanics. President of Connecticut river Navigation Association. Chairman of the executive board of the Good Government club. On committee on harbors and public lands in House of 1897-8.

Vote of district: Charles E. Hoag, Republican, 614; S. M. Jones, Democrat, 529.

District No. 6.—Wards 1, 2, 3, 4, 5, 6 of Chicopee.—DANIEL J. DRISCOLL, Democrat, of Chicopee, was born in that city Nov. 20, 1868; public schools. Bicycle polisher. Common council, 1895-6. Foresters, Father Mathew T. A. M. B.; metal polishers' and platers' union, secretary two years, president one.

Vote of district: H. J. Boyd, Republican, 626; Daniel J. Driscoll, Democrat, 815.

District No. 7.—Ward 7 of Chicopee, Wards 1, 2, 3, 4, 5 of Holyoke.—THOMAS J. DOOLING, Democrat, of Holyoke was born in that city Jan. 28, 1868; public schools. Is a "beamer." Fire department; local clubs. Committee on fisheries and game, House 1897; election laws, 1898.

JOHN F. SHEEHAN, Democrat, of Holyoke was born in that city, Sept. 2, 1864. Prominent in social and literary clubs. Law student. Committee on cities, and on woman suffrage in House of 1895; cities, 1896; on same also in 1897-8.

Vote of district: Thomas J. Dooling, Democrat, 1259; G. Geissler, Socialist Labor, 209; F. Gervais, Republican, Democrat Independent N. P., 833; R.

W. Hunter, Republican, 662 ; M. E. Ruther, Socialist Labor, 297 ; John F. Sheehan, Democrat, 1428.

District No. 8.—Wards 6, 7 of Holyoke.—ASHTON E. HEMPHILL, Republican, Holyoke, born in Acworth, N. H., Sept. 17, 1849; public schools, College of Pharmacy. Drug business ; storage business ; civil service board. State committee, 1890-2. Home Market, Mass. Republican clubs. House of 1881, printing committee; 1885, chairman of same, and on public health ; liquor law, mercantile affairs, 1898.

Vote of district: Ashton E. Hemphill, Republican, 753; J. O'Shea, Democrat, 493.

District No. 9.—Blandford, Chester, Montgomery, Russell, West Springfield, Westfield.—S. AUGUSTUS ALLEN of Westfield, Democrat, was born in that town, Feb. 14, 1853; public schools, Wesleyan Academy and Connecticut Literary Institute. Has been farmer, merchant and manufacturer ; now general manager of the Great River Water Power Company. President of First national bank ; trustee of Woronoco savings bank. Assessor in 1882. House of 1896, committee on water supply ; on committee on insurance, 1898.

ANDREW CAMPBELL, Republican, of Westfield, was born in New York, May 3, 1826 ; educated in public schools. Enlisted Aug. 29, 1862, in Co. C. 46th regiment Mass. Volunteers, served at Newbern, N. C., promoted to captain, mustered out July 29, 1863. Member of G. A. R. post 41, and commander of same; Loyal Legion. Special county commissioner in 1872. Republican town committee. United States store keeper, 1872-3-4. Is a painter. Member of Mount Moriah lodge of Masons. On committee on military affairs in House of 1897-8.

Vote of district : S Augustus Allen, Democrat, 1357 ; Andrew Campbell, Republican, 1338; J. H. Keefe, Democrat, 901 ; F. P. Sargent, Republican, 1115.

HAMPSHIRE COUNTY.

District No. 1.—Goshen, Hadley, Hatfield, Northampton, Westhampton, Williamsburg.—CHARLES S. CROUCH, Republican, of Northampton, was born in Wardsboro, Vt., Aug. 27, 1833 ; educated in public and private schools of Brattleboro, Vt., and of Springfield and Chicopee, Mass. For many years was a contractor, builder and dealer in real estate. Member of common council in 1890-1 ; board of aldermen 1893-4. Charter member, director and on finance committee of Northampton co-operative bank ; also charter member of Hampshire county savings bank of Northampton. On committee on public charitable institutions in House of 1898.

JOHN W. HILL of Williamsburg, Republican, was born in that town, July 1, 1846, and was educated in the public schools, and Wesleyan Academy of Wilbraham. Is a manufacturer. Junior warden of Hampshire lodge of Masons, and Williamsburg lodge Knights of Pythias. On committees on education, and parishes and religious societies, 1898.

Vote of district : G. H. Ames, Prohibition, 118 ; Charles S. Crouch, Republican, 495 ; J. J. Egan, Democrat, 993 ; John W. Hill, Republican, 1278 ; L. M. Norton, Prohibition. 71 ; H. W. Warner, Democrat. 786.

District No. 2.—Chesterfield, Cummington, Easthampton, Huntington, Middlefield, Plainfield, Southampton, Worthington.—HORATIO BISBEE of Chesterfield, Republican, was born in that town, Nov. 20, 1833, and was educated in the public schools. Has been in the lumbering and manufacturing business, a dealer in grain, and a farmer, all of which branches of business he carries on at present. Selectman 1871-2. Trustee of Haydenville savings bank since 1895 ; director of Williamsburg creamery since 1893 ; director of Hillside agricultural society since 1886. Chairman of trustees, public library. On committee on agriculture, 1898.

Vote of district: Horatio Bisbee, Republican, 679; B. T. Wetherell, Democrat, 643.

District No. 3.—Amherst, Granby, Pelham, South Hadley.—HENRY E. GAYLORD of South Hadley (Falls), Republican, was born in that town, June 5, 1846; educated in the public schools and Hudson River Institute of Claverack, N. Y. Clerk in store and post office in South Hadley Falls till 1870, then in the grocery and provision business in Easthampton till 1872, and since then has been in the coal and wood business in Holyoke and South Hadley Falls. Assessor in 1885-6-7; selectman in 1886-7, chairman; water commissioner for the past 20 years, and chairman. Is a 32d degree Mason. In House of 1895, on committee on public charitable institutions. Is a director in the Parsons paper company, the Valley paper company, and trustee of the Mechanics savings bank, and a member of the finance committee, all in Holyoke; and is president of the South Hadley Falls electric light company. On committee on roads and bridges, 1898.

Vote of district: Henry E. Gaylord, Republican, 784; all others, 8.

District No. 4.—Belchertown, Enfield, Greenwich, Prescott, Ware.—WILLIAM W. NEWCOMB, Republican, of Ware, was born in Hardwick, July 23, 1865; educated in the public schools. Is a book-keeper and paymaster. Town auditor since 1892. Past master of Eden lodge of Masons, member of Ware lodge of Odd Fellows, of Ware lodge of A. O. U. W., of Sons of Veterans and of Northampton commandery of Knights Templar. On committee on prisons in House of 1898.

Vote of district: J. J. Kidgell, Democrat, 461; William H. Newcomb, Republican, 729.

MIDDLESEX COUNTY.

District No. 1.—Ward 1 of Cambridge.—JAMES J. MYERS, Republican, was born near Frewsburg, N. Y., where his grandparents on both sides were among the pioneer settlers. On his father's side they were the old Mohawk Dutch stock of Myers and Van Valkenburgh; and on his mother's, the New England stock of Tracy and Stevens. He still owns the farm where he was born, and it has been in the family ever since it was bought by his grandfather of the Holland Land Company early in the century. While fitting for college, engaged more or less in the lumbering business for several years in the Alleghany and Ohio Rivers. Graduated at Harvard, 1869; at Harvard Law School, 1872. While in law school, taught mathematics one year in Harvard College. Spent one year in Europe and one year in a law office in New York city before beginning practice in Boston. In the fall of 1874, with J. B. Warner of Cambridge formed the partnership of Myers & Warner, and has ever since been engaged in the practice of the law in Boston, residing in Cambridge. President for one year of the Library Hall association of Cambridge. For two years president of the Colonial club of Cambridge; member of the University club, the Union club, the St. Botolph club and the Merchants' club of Boston; also of the Middlesex club, the Massachusetts club, the Massachusetts Republican club, the Massachusetts Reform club, the Cambridge club and the Cambridge Citizens' trade association; also a member of the Century association, the University club and the Zeta Psi club of New York; for several years treasurer of the Cambridge branch of the Indian Rights association and for some years member of the executive committee of the Cambridge Civil Service Reform association. Member of committees on probate and insolvency, elections and rules, and on recess committee on revision of corporation laws, in House of 1893; House chairman of special committee on revision of corporation laws, rules and judiciary, 1894; House chairman of committee on judiciary, and on rules, 1895; House chairman of committee on judiciary and on rules, 1896; same positions in House of 1897; same positions in 1898.

Vote of district: J. C. Daley, Democrat, 352; James J. Myers, Republican, 933.

District No. 2.—Ward 2 of Cambridge.—WILLIAM R. DAVIS, Republican, was born in West Appleton, Me., March 8, 1862; educated in the public schools. Is in the cooperage department of the J. P. Squire corporation. Member of common council, 1894-5-6. Member of Commercial lodge of Odd Fellows, Boston; Cambridge lodge of N. E. O. P.; and J. C. Wellington camp of Sons of Veterans; Citizens' trade association of Cambridge; Republican city committee, 1894-5-6; chairman of Ward 2 Republican committee, 1896-7. On committee on libraries and liquor law in House of 1897; on street railways, 1898.

JAMES MONTGOMERY, of Cambridge, Democrat, was born in that city, May 17, 1864; public schools. Salesman. Knights of Pythias; Red Men; Pilgrim Fathers; Cambridge Catholic Union; treasurer of Cambridge Tammany Club. On committee on water supply, 1898.

Vote of district: J. F. Aylward, 1066; William R. Davis, Republican, 1258; James A. Montgomery, Democrat, 1289; C. H. Titus, Republican, 1126.

District No. 3.—Ward 3 of Cambridge.—JOHN H. PONCE, Democrat, of Cambridge, was born in (East) Cambridge, Nov. 1, 1857; educated in public schools, Holy Cross College, Harvard and Boston University law schools; was reporter on Cambridge weeklies and Boston dailies; admitted to the bar in 1881, and has practiced law in Boston and Cambridge since. Secretary and attorney of Cambridge co-operative bank since 1882. Served in common council in 1892, and in aldermen in 1893-4; as alderman had largest number of committees and chairmanships; on committee on finance three years, being first named of committee while alderman; as councilman, introduced the order which led to present park system of the city, receiving from chairman of park commission the gold pen used by the mayor in signing the orders for taking of lands for parks. Associate member of post 57, G. A. R.; member of First Volunteers citizens' association, Charitable Irish Society. Father Mathew Total Abstinence Society, St. John's Literary Institute, Division 15 A. O. H., Lechmere council of Royal Arcanum; president of Columbus association; president of Lechmere cycle club, L. A. W.; grand knight of St. John's council, No. 193, Knights of Columbus; member of finance committee of citizens' committee on celebration of 50th anniversary of incorporation of city. Clerk of committee on public charitable institutions; also on special committee of Legislature to attend the dedication of the monument to John Boyle O'Reilly in Back Bay Fens, June 20, 1896; on committee on railroads, 1897; on same committee, 1898.

Vote of district: P. B. Bleiler, Republican, 359; John H. Ponce, Democrat, 827.

District No. 4.—Ward 4 of Cambridge.—DANIEL S. COOLIDGE, of Cambridge, Republican, born in Sherborn, Sept. 21, 1845; public schools. For 18 years with Mason & Hamlin Organ Company, but for the last 12 years has been one of the proprietors of the Bay State laundry of Cambridge. "No license" campaign committee 1892-5; on Republican city committee since 1893, treasurer of same 1895; common council, 1895-6-7. On committee on public charitable institutions, 1898.

CHARLES P. KEITH, of Cambridge, Republican, born in Newport, N. H., March 14, 1843; public schools. Enlisted Dec. 9, 1861, in Co. B. 1st regiment, mustered out Feb. 3, 1863; G. A. R. Manufacturer of brooms and brushes; real estate and insurance. Common council 1893-4. Masons, K. T. Committee on metropolitan affairs, 1898.

Vote of district: Daniel S. Coolidge, Republican, 1067; J. Corkery, Democrat, 424; Charles P. Keith, Republican, 1154.

District No. 5.—Ward 5 of Cambridge.—ALBERT S. APSEY of Cambridge, Republican, was born in that city, Nov. 27, 1870, and was educated in the public schools, Harvard College 1893, and Harvard Law School 1895. Is a lawyer with offices in Cambridge and No. 5, Tremont street, Boston. Member of common council 1895-6-7, being president in 1897. Member of Charity lodge of Masons, of Cambridge Republican city committee, of the Economy club, of Citizens' trade association, and of Young Men's Republican club. On committees on bills in 3d reading, and probate and insolvency, 1898.

Vote of district: Albert S. Apsey, Republican, 632; G. E. McNeill, Democrat, 258.

District No. 6.—Ward 1 of Somerville.—HORACE C. WHITE, Republican, was born in Bowdoin, Me., Jan. 26, 1836; educated in Litchfield Liberal Institute and the medical department of Bowdoin College in the class of 1859. Enlisted March 13, 1862, as assistant surgeon of the 8th Maine regiment and served in the Deparment of the South; mustered out in June, 1863. Member of Willard C. Kinsley post 139 G. A. R.; also of Loyal Legion. A teacher until 1860, and since a physician and surgeon. On Somerville school board from 1880 to 1892, a trustee and president of medical board of Somerville hospital for the last four years. Past master of Ancient York lodge of Masons of Lisbon, Me.; member of Soley lodge, of Orient council, and of DeMolay commandery of Masons; also member of Excelsior council No. 3 of Royal Arcanum, and of Mt. Benedict lodge of Knights of Honor. President of Mystic Valley club. Member of Massachusetts medical society, of American medical association, ex-president of Boston gynecological society, and of Somerville medical society. On committee on metropolitan affairs in House of 1897; on same committee, 1898.

Vote of district: C. D. Baker, Democrat, 209; Horace C. White, Republican, 601.

District No. 7.—Wards 2, 4 of Somerville.—FRANKLIN E. HUNTRESS, Republican, born in Biddeford, Me., April 19, 1866. Harvard college, class of 1889. In iron and steel business. Common council 1892-4. Member of Masons, Odd Fellows, Royal Arcanum. On committee on manufactures in House of 1897; on same in 1898.

MELVILLE D. JONES, Republican, born in Boston, Sept. 25, 1842; public schools. Enlisted in 1861 for three months in Co. D, 5th regiment; in 1862 for nine months in Co. F, 6th. G. A. R.; Masons, K. T. Ornamental iron goods business. On committees on elections, and printing, House of 1897; on counties, and State House, 1898.

FRANKLIN F. PHILLIPS, Republican, born in Searsmont, Me., Dec. 2, 1852; Bates College, class of 1877. Principal of Rockland, Me., High school 1878-83; state assayer of Maine 1880-40; chemist and chemical agent, 1883-98. Common council 1891-2; aldermen, 1893-4. Masons. On public service committee in House of 1897; House chairman of committee on public service, and on education, 1898.

Vote of district: D. W. Bennett, Republican Citizens N. P., 720; W. H. Berry, Republican Independent N. P., 787; L. F. Cook, Republican Citizens' N. P., 602; J. C. Cummings, Democrat, 464; Franklin E. Huntress, Republican, 1351; Melville D. Jones, Republican, 1411; A. F. Pecheur, Socialist Labor, 75; T. M. Nolan, Democrat, 475; I. S. Perry, Democrat Independent N. P., 132; Franklin F. Phillips, Republican, 1240; I. F. Symonds, Democrat, 546.

District No. 8.—Ward 3 of Somerville.—LEONARD B CHANDLER, Republican, was born in Princeton, Aug. 29, 1851; educated in the public schools. In the milk business. Member of common council in 1893-4; of aldermen in 1895-6. Member of John Abbott lodge of Masons, and of Coeur de Lion commandery of Knights Templar. Past grand of Paul Revere lodge of Odd Fellows. On committee on taxation in House of 1897; on committee on public charitable institutions, 1898

Vote of district: R. F. Baker, Democrat, 241; Leonard B. Chandler, Republican, 1086.

District No. 9—Wards 1, 2, 4, 5 of Medford—J. GILMAN WAITE, Republican; born March 20, 1836; public schools. School teacher; book-keeper; accountant. Medford school committee 1873-93 consecutively; board of commissioners of sinking funds since 1878; clerk of Medford savings bank since 1875 and trustee since 1881. Masons. On committee on ways and means of the House of 1897; on same committee, 1898.

Vote of district: J. C. Gillis, Democrat, 242; J. Gilman Waite, Republican, 681.

District No. 10.—Everett.—AMOS E. HALL, Republican, was born in Marshfield, Vt., July 8, 1838; educated in Morrisville (Vt.) Academy. In mercantile business for eight years, but has been in insurance and real estate business for 30 years. Park commissioner of Everett in 1893-4-5-6-7-8, being first appointed for three years and then re-appointed for five; chairman of board in 1894-5 6. Chairman of Prohibition state committee, 1886; Prohibition candidate for secretary of state, 1887. A Mason. In Odd Fellows, recording secretary six years, noble grand, past grand, representative to grand lodge. On committee on towns in House of 1897; clerk of same, and on banks and banking, 1898.

H. HEUSTIS NEWTON of Everett, Republican, was born in Truro, Dec. 2, 1860; educated in the public schools of Chatham and Provincetown, and in Boston University class of 1883. Taught school for 12 years in the towns of Essex, West Newbury, and Wellfleet, Mass.; has practiced law for the last five years in Boston and Everett; office in Tremont building, Boston. Admitted to the bar in Barnstable county, 1886. Member of Everett school committee 1892-3-4-5 6; private secretary of Mayor A. H. Evans, 1892; city solicitor, 1895-6-7-8. Member of Adams lodge of Masons, Wellfleet, and of Royal Arch of Provincetown; regent of Wellfleet council of Royal Arcanum; member of colony of Pilgrim Fathers. On committee on judiciary, 1898.

Vote of district: Amos E. Hall, Republican, 1025; C. Manser, Republican Citizens N. P., 886; H. Heustis Newton, Republican, 1101.

District No. 11.—Malden.—HARVEY L. BOUTWELL, Republican, of Malden was born in Meredosia, Ill., April 5, 1860; educated in public schools and New Hampshire state college, class of 1882. Principal of Claremont, N. H., grammar school, 1882-3. Graduate of Boston University law school, 1886; practiced law in Boston since then. Principal of Eliot evening school in Boston for ten years. Member of Malden lodge of Odd Fellows. A. O. U. W., Republican club of Mass., Middlesex Club, Malden board of trade, Marketmen's Republican club, Malden club; United Order of Golden Cross, representing the latter to supreme commandery in 1890, honorary vice president of Convocation of Boston University. Member of common council, 1893-4. Clerk of committee on metropolitan affairs in House of 1895; on committees on constitutional amendments, and metropolitan affairs (clerk), and House chairman of the committee on redistricting the state, 1896; House chairman of committee on manufactures, 1897; same position in 1898, and also on committee on insurance.

CHARLES L. DEAN, Republican, was born in Ashford, Conn., May 29, 1844. At 16, he entered the employ of the Westford glass company of that town, and at 21 became a member of the firm of E. A. Buck & Co., glass manufacturers. In

1871, July 17, he engaged in business at 14 Blackstone street, Boston, and has been there ever since, having been from October 15, 1874, senior member of the firm of Dean, Foster & Co. manufacturers of glassware and druggists' sundries, one of the largest firms in New England in their line. Appointed post master at Westford, Conn. at 21, and held the office for 12 years; at 25, he was offered the position of deputy sheriff of Windham county, but declined it. County commissioner of Windham county, Conn., for six years from 1869, being only 25 years of age, and the youngest man that has ever held the position in that state. In 1879-80 was senior aid on the staff of Gov Andrews of Conn., this giving him the rank of colonel. In 1881-2 he was member of the House of Representatives of Connecticut, serving on important committees In 1885, he changed his residence from Connecticut to Malden, and has since resided there. Member of the common council in 1892-93; and of the board of aldermen in 1894-5-6, being chairman of the latter in 1896, and a member of the finance committee, the last four of his five years in the city government. President of the First national bank of Stafford Springs, Conn., and one of the stock holders of the Warren woolen company of that place; one of the incorporators and vice president of the Malden trust company, and director of the Malden co-operative savings bank; was one of the incorporators, and is a trustee and a member of the finance committee of the Malden hospital. On his twelfth year as a trustee of the Centre Methodist Episcopal church of Malden. Was a member of the committee that built the Y. M. C. A. building in Malden, and chairman of the finance committee. Member of committee on ways and means in House of 1897; on same committee, 1898.

JOHN A. POWERS, Republican, of Malden, born in Boston, Sept. 15, 1853; public schools. Plumbing, gas fitting, hardware business. Common council 1891-2; aldermen, 1893-4. Masons, 32d degree; Knights of Pythias. On committee on drainage in House of 1897; House chairman of same committee, 1898

Vote of district: F. S. Atwood, Democrat 485; Harvey L. Boutwell, Republican, 1899; Charles L. Dean, Republican, 2022; J. H. Gray, Prohibition, 163; W. F. Merrill, Prohibition, 534; H. F. Pickering, Prohibition, 150; John A. Powers, Republican, 1774; J. C. Robinson, Republican Citizens, N. P., 1176.

District No. 12.—Wards 3, 6 of Medford, Winchester.—JOHN FULLER LIBBY of Medford, Republican, was born in Richmond, Me., Feb. 3. 1863; educated in public schools and Bowdoin College, class of 1885. Principal of Waldoboro (Me.,) High school, 1885 7; associate principal of Bridgton Academy, North Bridgton, Me., 1887-8; studied law in the office of Symonds & Libby, Portland, Me., while engaged in teaching, and of Attorney General Charles E. Littlefield, of Rockland, Me., 1888-90; admitted to the bar in March, 1890, and practiced in Rockland, Me., until July, 1892, when he removed to Boston, where his office is at No. 15 Court Square. Member of Rockland common council, 1891-2, being president in 1892; secretary and treasurer of the Public Library association from time of its organization until 1892; member of Rockland school board, 1890-2; member of Ligonia lodge No. 5 of Portland, Me., Odd Fellows; of Mystic encampment of Medford; of the Bowdoin club of Boston. Director of Medford club, Medford; member of Medford education society, Medford historical society; mayor's clerk of Medford, 1897-8. On committee on probate and insolvency in House of 1898.

Vote of district: J. T. Cosgrove, Democrat, 239; John F. Libby, Republican, 877.

District No. 13.—Arlington, Lexington.—GEORGE F. MEAD, Republican, of Lexington, born in Roxbury, May 22. 1854; Somerville High school. Member of commission house of J. D. Mead & Co., Boston; Boston Chamber of Commerce Fruit & Produce Exchange; Boston associated board of trade; Boston

Marketmen's Republican club; Republican club of Massachusetts; Middlesex club; Royal Arcanum, Knights of Honor; Mason. On committee on metropolitan affairs in House of 1897; clerk of same committee, 1898.

Vote of district: George F. Mead, Republican, 764; all others, 15.

District No. 14—Belmont, Watertown.—FRED E. CRAWFORD, Republican, Watertown; born in Guildhall, Vt., July, 7, 1857; Harvard College, 1881. Attorney-at-law. Committees on constitutional amendments, probate and insolvency, House, 1897; chairman committee on bills in 3d reading, and on labor, 1898.

Vote of district: Fred E. Crawford, Republican, 764; all others, 15.

District No. 15.—Waltham.—OTIS M. GOVE, Republican, was born in Seabrook, N. H., May 3, 1851; educated in the public schools and Oak Grove Seminary of Vassalboro, Me. Was a photographer until 1883, when he retired. Treasurer of Republican city committee for 1891-2-3-4-5-6-7 S. Member of aldermen in 1892-3. Past grand of Independent lodge of Odd Fellows and its treasurer for the last seven years, member of Monitor lodge, Waltham royal arch chapter and Gethsemane commandery of Masons; member of O. E. S. M. P. A.; past patron of Electa chapter O E. S. Member of Waltham savings bank corporation. On committee on railroads in House of 1897; on same committee, and on banks and banking, 1898.

GEORGE W. WHIDDEN, Republican, was born in South Danvers (now Peabody,) June 15, 1858; educated in the public schools and Westford Academy. Is in the railroad business. Member of Waltham school committee 1892-3-4-5. Past grand of Prospect lodge and member of Waltham encampment of Odd Fellows. Member of committees on State House, and taxation in House of 1897; House chairman of former, and clerk of latter, 1898.

Vote of district: Otis M. Gove, Republican, 1449; George W. Whidden, Republican, 1367; all others, none.

District No. 16.—Newton—ALBERT F. HAYWARD, Republican, of Newton, was born in Bridgewater, January 24, 1840; educated in the public schools. Is a manufacturer of confectionery in Boston, being president and treasurer of Fobes, Hayward & Co (incorporated.) President of the Puritan trust company of Boston; vice president of Newton Centre trust company, and trustee of Newton Centre savings bank. Member of advisory board National Association of manufacturing confectioners. On committee on banks and banking in House of 1897; on ways and means, 1898.

EDWARD L. PICKARD, Republican, of Newton, was born in Lewiston, Me., Dec. 25, 1834; educated in the public schools and Lewiston Academy of Auburn, Me. In the boot and shoe manufacturing business from the age of 14 to 26; in the hide and leather business, partner of N. W. Rice, since March 12, 1860, to the present time. Member of common council in 1870-1. On committee on metropolitan affairs in House of 1897, and also of 1898.

Vote of district: Albert F. Hayward, Republican, 2036; C. S. Morris, Prohibition, 240; Edward L. Pickard, Republican, 2092.

District No. 17.—Bedford, Concord, Lincoln, Weston.—CHARLES E. BROWN Republican, of Concord, was born in that town, Nov. 18, 1850; educated in the public schools and a Boston commercial college. Has been in the wholesale and retail dry goods business. Town treasurer, 1883-4-5; chairman of selectmen, 1887-8; water commissioner, 1883-4-5-7-8; auditor, 1889-90-1; town clerk, 1894-5-6-7. Trustee and member of investment committee of Middlesex institution for savings; director of Concord national bank; director in American Powder Mills. Past master of Corinthian lodge of Masons; past high priest Walden chapter, life member Boston commandery of Knights Templar; past district deputy grand master of 11th district. Member of Massachusetts Republican club,

also Middlesex club. Clerk of committee on insurance, 1897; House chairman of same committee, 1898.
Vote of district: Charles E. Brown, 536; all others, five.

District No. 18.—*Natick.*—FRANCIS C. PERRY, Republican, of Natick, was born in that town, June 27, 1853; educated in the public schools. Railroad; real estate and insurance business. Member of the school board in 1894-5 6; overseer of the poor in 1895-6 7-8. Member of Meridian lodge of Masons; and a member of other social and fraternal organizations. On committee on insurance, 1897; clerk of insurance, and on State House, 1898.

District No. 19. *Ashland, Holliston, Hopkinton, Sherborn*—ZEPHANIAH TALBOT of Holliston, Republican, was born in (South) Hanover, June 22, 1834, and was educated in the public schools and Hanover Academy. Entered the United States naval service, May 3, 1859, as staff officer in the line of promotion; was promoted to 1st assistant engineer. Member of Powell T. Wyman post No. 6 G. A. R. During the war was chief engineer on the steam gunboats Chocura and Iosco, superintending the placing in them of their engines at Charlestown, and then holding this position on the Iosco at the close of the war. Took part in both bombardments and capture of Fort Fisher. Assistant professor of steam engineering at Annapolis Naval Academy 1865-6, and since then in the manufacture of tacks, mostly at Holliston. On board of selectmen in 1886-96-7; assessor in 1875, and chairman of board in 1876-7. On school committee 1876-84-86 to '91, as chairman and secretary. For several years on board of investment of Holliston savings bank, and now on auditing committee. President of Holliston national bank since spring of 1896. Treasurer of Holliston mills 1882-8, when he was unanimously made trustee to wind up their affairs. Member of Mt. Hollis lodge of Masons; chancellor commander of Winthrop lodge of Knights of Pythias in Holliston. On committee on taxation, 1898.
Vote of district: F. Cass, Democrat, 656; Zephaniah Talbot, Republican, 693.

District No. 20.—*Framingham.*—CHARLES DUDLEY LEWIS, Democrat, of Framingham, was born in Roxbury (Boston), Sept. 26, 1844; educated in public and private schools. Was engaged in mercantile business for many years, as a member of the firm of A. S. & W. G. Lewis & Co., of Boston; and in later years in farming. For many years treasurer of the Democratic state central committee; member of national Democratic committee in 1888-92; delegate to several national Democratic conventions during the past 20 years; now member of Democratic state committee at large. On committee on banks and banking in House of 1898.
Vote of district: Charles Dudley Lewis, 814; J. M. Merriam, Republican, 751.

District No. 21.—*Marlboro, Sudbury, Wayland.*—GEORGE BALCOM of Marlboro, Democrat, was born in Concord, Mass., Jan. 23, 1832, and was educated in the Cambridge public schools. Enlisted in August, 1862, in Co. I, 5th regiment, served in North Carolina, where he was seriously injured in the line of the duty at Hamilton; promoted to be sergeant and mustered out of service July 2, 1863. Member of John A. Rawlins post No. 43, Marlboro, G. A. R. Has been shoemaker, manufacturer and dealer, and is now janitor. Chief of Marlboro fire department. Captain of militia in 1865-6. Chancellor commander of Marlboro lodge of Knights of Pythias, and member of grand lodge of Massachusetts. On committee on drainage, 1898.

WILLIAM L. MORSE, Republican, of Marlboro was born in that city, May 1, 1849; educated in the public schools, Phillips Exeter Academy, Harvard College class of 1874. Merchant since 1874, member of firm of Morse & Bigelow of Marlboro since 1876. Serving sixteenth consecutive year on school board. Director of First national bank, trustee of the savings bank, both of Marlboro. A civil service examiner for the city. Trustee of the Massachusetts Homeopathic hospital of Boston. On committee on education in House of 1897; clerk of same committee, 1898.

Vote of district: George Balcom, Democrat, 1334; D. Brackett, Republican, 1095; R. T Lombard, Democrat, 919; William L. Morse, Republican, 1354.

District No. 22.—Boxborough, Hudson, Maynard, Stow.—RUFUS HOWE, Republican, Hudson, born in Bolton, Sept. 28, 1837; public schools. Enlisted in Co. I, 36th regiment, Aug. 1862; mustered out June, 1865. Commander of Reno post No. 9, G. A. R. three years; Masons. Shoe cutter. Committee on taxation, 1897; on parishes and religious societies, and towns, 1898.

Vote of district: Rufus Howe, Republican, 777; all others, 10.

District No. 23.—Acton, Ayer, Littleton, Shirley, Westford.—FRANK H. WHITCOMB, Republican, of (West) Acton was born in Boxboro, Jan. 7, 1838; educated in the public schools. Enlisted Sept., 1862, in Co. E. 6th regiment and served in Suffolk, Va., promoted to 1st sergeant and captain; mustered out Nov. 1863. Member of Isaac Davis post No. 138 G. A. R., and its commander 1895-6-7 Is a farmer. On committee on public health, 1898.

Vote of district: Frank H. Whitcomb, Republican, 608; all others, six.

District No. 24.—Ashby, Groton, Pepperell, Townsend.—GEORGE L. WHITCOMB of Townsend (Center), Republican, was born in that town, March 18, 1855, and was educated in public and private schools. Is a farmer. On school committee since 1888; member of Townsend Grange since it was organized in 1888. Member of House in 1896, chairman of committee on agriculture. On committees on parishes and religious societies, and on taxation, 1898.

Vote of district: U. W. Kidder, Democrat, 188; George L. Whitcomb, Republican, 550.

District No. 25.—Chelmsford, Dunstable, Wards 4, 7, 8 of Lowell, Tyngsboro—WILLIAM H. I. HAYES, Republican, of Lowell, was born in Boston, June 21, 1848. His mother removed to Lowell in 1849, his father going to California, where he died. When eight years old, removed to Groton, going on a farm at eleven, and to school only in the winter. When only thirteen, enlisted in Company B of the Sixth Regiment, under call for one-hundred days men. Spent three days at Faneuil Hall, then returned, April, 1863, as call was changed for three years. In August, 1862, enlisted in Company B, Sixth Regiment, and served in Peck's division, Seventh Army Corps, in Suffolk and Norfolk, Va. Here gained the nickname of "Old Hundred", he was so young and small, being one of the very youngest soldiers who carried a gun. Mr. Hayes comes of fighting stock. His grandfather was in the Mexican War; his great-grandfather on his mother's side was at the battle of Bunker Hill; while his great-great-grandfather was Capt. Oliver Parker, in the same fight. The mother of Capt. Oliver Parker did her part also in the struggle against the Indians of those days, of whom she is said to have killed three, who attacked her house in the absence of its male defenders. Having served his first enlistment, he re-enlisted in November, 1863, in Company B of the Fifty-sixth regiment, and served all through Grant's campaigns, and was finally mustered out at Readville, July, 1865. Is president of Association of Survivors of Company B, Sixth Regiment which members always meets September 15, anniversary of their arrival at Suffolk; also of Association of Survivors of Fifty-sixth Regiment, which meets annually, May 6, anniversary of the battle of the Wilderness. After war, made cigars and travelled as salesman until going into business for himself in 1877, now being a manufacturer of cigars and wholesale dealer in the same, making a specialty of the "Old Hundred" brand named after the nickname given him while in the army. Is member and past commander of B. F. Butler Post, G. A. R.; also of the Red Men, Odd Fellows, Knights of Pythias, and Masons. Director of Home Guaranty insurance company, and of Middlesex trust company of Lowell On committees on elections and liquor law in House of 1893; committees on insurance, and water supply in House of 1894; committees on street railways, and water supply, 1895; House chairman of committee on State House, and on water supply, 1896; House chairman of committee on cities, and on rules, 1897; same positions, 1898.

WILLIAM A. LANG, Republican, of Lowell, was born in Limerick, Me., May 26, 1836, educated in public and private schools. Teacher and chaplain of reform school and institutions of Lowell for 35 years. Member of common council, 1885-6. Member of Masons and Knights Templar, also member of Scottish Rite 32d degree; chaplain of Ancient York lodge for the past 30 years; chaplain of Mt. Horeb royal arch chapter and Ahasuerus council for the past 25 years. Committee on fisheries and game in House of 1897; on same committee, and on roads and bridges, 1898.

JAMES P. RAMSAY, Republican, of Lowell, born in Arbroath, Scotland, April 30, 1861; public schools. Is engaged in steam railroading. Masons. Odd Fellows. On committee on public service in House of 1897; clerk of public service, and on State House, 1898.

Vote of district: G. O. Byam, Democrat, 1551; W. H. I. Hayes. Republican, 2064; William A. Lang, Republican, 2013; J. P. Mahoney, Democrat, 1497; James P. Ramsay, Republican, 2043; C. Whitman, Democrat, 1539.

District No. 26.—Ward 1, 2, 3, 6 of Lowell.—HENRY J. DRAPER, Democrat, of Lowell, was born in that city, March 5, 1857; educated in the public schools. Is a carriage painter. Captain of Admiral Farragut Post No. 78 Sons of Veterans. Member of common council in 1889. Member of Wamesit court of Foresters. On committee on counties in House of 1898.

JOSEPH E. PATTEE, Republican, was born in Thornton, N. H., April 24, 1843; educated in the public schools. Has been in the staging and hotel business. Has held various town offices of Lincoln and Thornton from 1870 to 1886. Member of the U. A. M.; of Lowell Republican city committee, 1894-5-6-7-8-9. On committee on prisons in House of 1897; on same committee in 1898.

EDWARD THOMAS ROWELL, Republican, was born in Concord, N. H., and passed his boyhood days upon the farm. He graduated at Dartmouth College in 1861. Enlisted as a private soldier in the Fifth N. H. regiment of volunteers in August, 1861, was commissioned second lieutenant in Co. F. 2d regiment, Berdan's United States sharpshooters and promoted to captain and major of his regiment and served until the close of the war. Has been in the newspaper business at Lowell since the war and is now president of the Courier-Citizen company, and president of the Railroad national bank. On committee on manufactures in House of 1897; on manufactures, and street railways, 1898.

Vote of district: R. Dobbins, Republican, 2052; Henry J. Draper, Democrat, 2097; J. G. Gordon, Democrat, 1860; J. F. McCarty, Democrat, 1858; Joseph E. Pattee, Republican, 2087; Edward T. Rowell, Republican, 2097.

District No. 27.—Billerica, Burlington, Carlisle, Dracut, Wards 5, 9 of Lowell, North Reading, Tewksbury, Wilmington.—BUTLER AMES, Republican, of Lowell was born in that city, Aug. 22, 1871, son of Gen. Adelbert Ames and grandson of Gen. Benj. F. Butler; educated in Phillips Exeter Academy, graduating from United States military academy as 2d lieutenant, 11th United States Infantry in 1894 and from the Massachusett Institute of Technology as a B. B.

in mechanical engineering in 1896. Member of Lowell common council in 1897. Senior 1st lieutenant of Battery A M. V. M. Agent of Wamesit power company. On committees on harbors and public lands, and military affairs in House of 1898. On May 17, was granted leave of absence at his own request for the remainder of the session, having been appointed adjutant of the "Old Sixth" regiment, which was subsequently sent to "the front," after being in camp at South Framingham, Mass., and at Falls Church, near Washington, D. C.

FRANK H. FARMER, Republican, of Tewksbury, born in that town, Oct. 13, 1857; public schools, Lowell Commercial College. Wood, coal, fire insurance business. Been town treasurer, assessor, overseer of poor, member of board of health. Odd Fellows. Committee on counties, 1898.

Vote of district: Butler Ames, Republican, 1673; J. G. Duffy, Democrat, 1303; Frank H. Farmer, Republican, 1621; J. P. O'Hare, Democrat, 1255.

District No. 28.—Reading, Woburn.—JAMES WILSON GRIMES, Republican, of Reading, was born in Hillsborough, N. H., Nov. 21, 1865; educated at Phillips Academy, Andover, and Boston University Law School, 1890. Admitted to bar in DesMoines, Ia., 1890. Member of Suffolk bar and Boston bar association, practicing in Boston. Member of Good Samaritan lodge of Masons, Middlesex and Massachusetts Republican clubs. On committee on probate and insolvency, and clerk of committee on printing in House of 1897; House chairman of roads and bridges, and on constitutional amendments in 1898.

ALVA SYLVANUS WOOD, Republican, of Woburn, was born in that city, May 12, 1828; educated in public and private schools and Warren Academy in the class of 1847. Has been engaged in the shoe manufacturing business, a railroad agent, book-keeper, and accountant. Past master of Mt. Horeb lodge of Masons; past high priest of Woburn royal arch chapter; member of Hugh de Payens commandery of Knights Templar of Melrose; 32d degree A. & A. Scottish Rite. Member of Sons of American Revolution and of Society of Colonial Wars. On committees on engrossed bills, and libraries in House of 1897; chairman of committee on engrossed bills, and clerk of prisons, 1898.

Vote of district: M. DeArcy, Democrat, 914; James Wilson Grimes, Republican, 1522; M. J. Meagher, Democrat, 932; Alva S. Wood, Republican, 1580.

District No. 29.—Wakefield.—CHARLES A. DEAN, Democrat, of Wakefield, was born in England; educated in the public schools. Has been engaged in the rattan business, and farming. Member of Wakefield board of assessors, of boards of finance and sewer committee; secretary of the public library; member of war relief committee in 1898; warden of Souhegan lodge of Odd Fellows. On committee on taxation in House of 1898, taking active part on taxation questions and introducing an inheritance tax bill, which was substituted for an adverse report and took two readings.

Vote of district: Charles A. Dean, Democrat, 733; O. V. Waterman, Republican, 610.

District No. 30.—Stoneham.—WILLIAM H. MARDEN, Republican, born in Charlestown, May 30, 1843. Served in Co. L, 6th regiment, and in 2d company of sharpshooters, in War of Rebellion. G. A. R. Farmer, shoe laster. Park commissioner. Committee on labor, House of 1895; labor, and military affairs, 1896; military affairs, and towns, 1897; House chairman of military affairs, and on towns, 1898.

Vote of district: William H. Marden, Republican, 645; all others, none.

District No. 31.—Melrose.—GEORGE R. JONES, Republican, born in Lebanon, Me.; educated in Melrose public schools; Boston University, and its law school, and with Allen, Long & Hemenway. Lawyer. On committees on constitutional amendments, and probate and insolvency in House of 1894; House chairman of metropolitan affairs, and on rules, 1895; same positions in 1896, 1897, 1898.

Vote of district: G. L. Davis, Democrat National Independent N. P., 199; George R. Jones, 997.

NANTUCKET COUNTY.

District No. 1.—Nantucket.—ROLLIN M. ALLEN, Republican, of Nantucket was born in East Bridgewater, April 10, 1862, and was educated in the Admiral Sir Isaac Coffin Academy in Nantucket preparatory for the United States Naval Academy, class of 1879. Was in the commission and is now engaged in general contracting business. Served as county commissioner since 1893 and as a selectman since 1893; also member of school committee. Past master of Union lodge of Masons, and member of Wanackneamack encampment of Odd Fellows. On committee on drainage, 1898.

Vote of district: Rollin M. Allen, Republican, 236; all others, 3.

NORFOLK COUNTY.

District No. 1.—Dedham, Norwood.—FRANCIS O. WINSLOW, Republican, of Norwood, was born in (South) Dedham (now Norwood) March 20, 1844; educated in public schools and Phillips Academy of Andover in the class of 1863. Retired from the firm of Winslow Brothers, wool pullers and sheep and goat leather manufacturers President of the Norwood co-operative bank since its organization; director in the Everett national bank of Boston for 15 years: treasurer of the state committee of the Young Men's Christian Associations of Massachusetts and Rhode Island. Member of the Congregational club. Chairman of Norwood school committee 1872-3. On committee on education in House of 1897; on mercantile affairs, and clerk of parishes and religious societies, 1898.

Vote of district: C. C. Sanderson, Democrat, 571; Francis O. Winslow, Republican, 900.

District No. 2.—Brookline.—JAMES M. CODMAN, Jr., of Brookline, Non-partisan, was born in that town, April 20, 1862, and was educated in private schools and Harvard College class of 1884. Is a lawyer. Member of selectmen and overseers of the poor and of the board of health in 1893-4-5-6-7-8. On committee on taxation, 1898.

Vote of district: James M. Codman, Jr., Non-partisan, 1026; E. B. Gibbs, Republican, 969.

District No. 3.—Hyde Park.—SAMUEL A. TUTTLE, Democrat, of Hyde Park was born in Effingham, N. H., Sept. 11, 1837; educated in the public schools and Wolfboro Academy. Is a veterinary surgeon and a manufacturer of "Tuttle's Elixir" and other veterinary remedies. Member of Hyde Park lodge of Masons, of Cyprus commandery, Tremont lodge of Odd Fellows. and of the Ancient and Honorable Artillery Company; also an associate member of the Grand Army post in Hyde Park. On committee on manufactures in House of 1898.

Vote of district: J. McKenna, Democrat Independent N. P., 34; Samuel A. Tuttle, Democrat, 767; L. P. Winchenbaugh, Republican, 735.

District No. 4.—Canton, Milton.—FREDERIC P. DRAKE of Canton, Republican, was born in Canton, March 16, 1851, and was educated in its public schools and Stoughtonham Institute of Sharon. Is a carpenter. On board of selectmen since 1892. Past noble grand of Blue Hill lodge of Odd Fellows, and its secretary for the past 11 years. On committee on federal relations, 1898.

Vote of district; Frederic P. Drake, Republican, 628; G. R. R. Rivers, Democrat, 615.

District No. 5.—Quincy.—THADDEUS H. NEWCOMB, Republican, of Quincy, was born in that city, March 15, 1826; educated in public and private schools. Enlisted as private Sept. 16, 1862, in Co. G. 42d regiment; mustered out as 1st lieutenant Sept 16, 1864. Member of Paul Revere post 88 G A. R. Member of common council 1889-90-1-2. Member of Adelphi lodge of Knights of Pythias. In House of 1896, on committee on liquor law; House chairman of same in 1897, and also in same position in 1898.

JAMES THOMPSON, Republican, of Quincy, was born in south of Scotland, May 18, 1848; came to this country in childhood. His ancestors in this country were among the earliest settlers in the Ohio Valley, establishing themselves upon the present site of Pittsburg, Pa. Educated in Quincy schools. Is a granite manufacturer. City council 1889-90 1 2, inclusive president in 1891-2. Mt. Wollaston lodge of Odd Fellows. A director of Granite national bank; an incorporator of Quincy savings bank; president of Granite Manufacturers' association, the product of whose quarries for monumental and building purposes is unsurpassed; vice president of Quincy board of trade. On committee on fisheries and game, 1896; on ways and means, 1897; same position, 1898.

Vote of district: Thaddeus H. Newcomb, Republican, 1314; J. H. Slade, Democrat, 756; James Thompson, Republican, 1358.

District No. 6.—Braintree, Weymouth.—MARTIN E. HAWES of (East) Weymouth, Republican, was born in that place, Oct. 25, 1834, and was educated in the public schools Has been a salesman, but is at present president of the Weymouth & Braintree Publishing Co, and associate manager and editor of its publications. Member of Orphans' Hope lodge of Masons, and its past master. President of the Fish and Game club of East Weymouth.

EDWARD B. NEVIN, Republican, of Weymouth was born in York, Penn., Nov. 10, 1858; educated in public schools. Is a wholesale coal dealer. Member of Columbian lodge of Masons, of Commonwealth lodge of Odd Fellows. On committee on railroads in House of 1897; on same committee, 1898.

Vote of district: Martin E. Hawes, Republican, 1022; Edward B. Nevin, Republican, 1143; H. F. Pierce, Democrat National, 191; J. B. Whelan, Democrat, 954.

District No. 7 —Avon, Holbrook, Randolph.—HENRY A. BELCHER, Republican of Randolph, was born in that town, Aug. 6, 1845; educated in the public schools. Partner in the firm of R. H. White & Co., of Boston for 19 years, retiring in 1896. On committee on mercantile affairs in House of 1897; House chairman of same committee, 1898.

Vote of district: Henry A. Belcher, Republican, 604; J. E. Foley, Democrat, 377.

District No. 8.—Sharon, Stoughton, Walpole.—WILLIAM CURTIS, Republican, of Stoughton was born in Charleston, S. C., Aug. 8, 1857; educated in the public schools. Is a Custom House broker; member of firm of Stone & Downer. Selectman in 1894-5. Past junior warden of Rising Star lodge of Masons. Associate member of A. St. John Chambre post No. 72, G. A. R. Member of A. O. U. W.; and chairman Republican town committee, Stoughton. Has been trustee of Stoughton public library, trustee of Rising Star lodge of Masons, vice president of Stoughton Historical and Antiquarian Society, secretary of Republican town committee and vice president of Commercial Club of Stoughton. On committee on banks and banking in House of 1897; House chairman of same committee, 1898.

Vote of district: William Curtis, Republican, 661; W. B. Wickes, Democrat, 210.

District No. 9.—Dover, Medfield, Millis, Needham, Wellesley.—ALBERT CLARKE, of Wellesley, (Wellesley Hills), Republican, was born in Granville, Vt., Oct. 13, 1840; educated in the public schools and Barre Academy, class of 1859; honorary degree of A. M. by Dartmouth College Enlisted Aug. 25, 1862, in 13th Vermont, serving until July 22, 1863. Commanded Company G at Gettysburg, where he was wounded; assisted in capturing cannon and prisoners, and in repulsing Pickett's charge. Member of Gettysburg post 191, G. A. R. of Boston; judge advocate of Dept. of Massachusetts, 1894; national judge advocate general, 1897; has been a lawyer, editor and publisher, and is now the secretary and executive officer of the Home Market club. Was 1st assistant clerk of Vermont House of Representatives, 1864-8; member of Vermont Senate, 1874; commissioner of state to build house of correction and monuments; president of Vermont & Canada railroad company; president of Rutland (Vt) board of trade; seven years president of Wellesley club; colonel on staff of Governor of Vermont, 1865; director of national prison association, 1874-8. Member of Massachusetts commandery of the Loyal Legion of the United States. Delegate to Republican national convention 1892. On committees on ways and means, rules and taxation, in House of 1896; on ways and means, and rules, 1897; House chairman of ways and means, and on rules, 1898.

Vote of district: Albert Clarke, Republican, 596; G. N. Smith, Democrat, 316.

District No 10.—Bellingham, Foxboro, Franklin, Medway, Norfolk, Wrentham.—ELBRIDGE J. WHITAKER, of Wrentham, was born in Wabaunsee, Kan., Nov. 11, 1859; educated in Amherst College class of 1883. Principal of Wrentham High school seven years. Is a lawyer with an office in Boston President of Norfolk county teachers' association for two years; town counsel 1896-8. Chairman of Republican town committee 1893 to 1898. Past master of Excelsior lodge of Masons; Past grand of Wampum lodge of Odd Fellows; and district deputy of the Odd Fellows. Member of House in 1895, clerk of committee on election laws. On judiciary committee, 1898.

GEORGE FENELON WILLIAMS of Foxboro, Republican, was born in Foxboro April 28, 1856, and was educated in the public schools and Chauncey-Hall school of Boston. In the express and railroad business for 15 years. Clerk of the water board from 1878 to the present. Town treasurer 1888-9; vice president of the Foxboro savings bank; president of the trustees of the Boyden public library for nine years. Chairman of the Republican town committee for last two years. Member of Excelsior lodge of Odd Fellows On committee on water supply, 1898

Vote of district: Elbridge J. Whitaker, Republican, 1016; George F. Williams, Republican, 991; all others, 16.

PLYMOUTH COUNTY.

District No. 1.—Kingston, Plymouth.—WILLIAM S. KYLE, of Plymouth, Republican, was born in 1851, and was educated in the public schools. Engaged in the wholesale drug business in Portland, Me., as clerk and partner for 21 years, and is now a manufacturer of insulated electrical wires at Plymouth, of the firm of Bradford, Kyle & Co. Member of Ancient Landmark lodge, of Mount Vernon chapter, and Portland (Me.) commandery of Knights Templar. President of the Commercial club; treasurer of the First parish and chairman of the Republican town committee On committee on mercantile affairs in House of 1898.

Vote of district: William S. Kyle, Republican, 675; L. G. Lanman, Democrat, 286.

District No. 2.—Duxbury, Marshfield, Norwell, Pembroke, Scituate.—WILLIAM A. JOSSELYN, Republican, of (North) Pembroke, was born, Feb. 8, 1856, in Rockland; educated in the public schools. Has been a boot and shoe cutter, and manufacturer of rands, 1894-5. Master of Phoenix lodge of Masons of Hanover; past grand of North River lodge No. 167 of Odd Fellows of Hanover, for several years has been permanent secretary of the same; district deputy of Mattabesett and Helping Hand lodges of Duxbury. On committees on street railways in House of 1897; on same committee, 1898.

Vote of district: J. J. Ford, Democrat, 102; William A. Josselyn, Republican, 397.

*District No. 3.—Cohassett, Hingham, Hull.—*EDWARD E WENTWORTH, Republican, of Cohasset, was born in Waterville, Me., July 27, 1845; educated in the public schools. Enlisted Dec. 15, 1861, in Co. F, 7th Maine regiment and served in the Army of the Potomac and in the Southwest; mustered out in 1864. Member of Henry Bryant post 98 G. A. R. and was its commander in 1889-92. Is a carriage manufacturer. Constable for 22 years and deputy sheriff for four years. Member of Konohasset lodge of Masons and of Cohassett lodge of Odd Fellows On committee on counties in House of 1898.

Vote of district: D. Daley. Democrat, 93; J. Reed, Prohibition 88; Edward E. Wentworth, Republican, 468.

*District No. 4.—Hanover, Hanson, Rockland.—*EBEN C. WATERMAN, Republican, of Hanover, was born in Scituate, (the part now Norwell), March 1, 1840; educated in the public schools, and a graduate of Hanover Academy, class of 1857. By trade a shipwright, having been the last apprentice to that trade on North River. Four years a clerk in the office of the naval constructor at Charlestown navy yard; since that time clerk, book-keeper, notary public, justice of the peace. Selectman, assessor and overseer of the poor of Hanover, first elected in 1889. Member of Old Colony commandery Knights Templar, and Pilgrim royal arch chapter of Abington; Phoenix lodge of Masons; North River lodge of Odd Fellows, and Fraternal commandery of Golden Cross of Hanover; and Rockland Colony of Pilgrim Fathers, of Rockland, having held various offices in each, and past presiding officer in all but the first two. Member of House of Representatives, 1891, serving on the committee on labor and as chairman in committee on engrossed bills. On committee on public charitable institutions of House of 1897; on same committee, and on public health, 1898.

Vote of district: I. Marks, Democrat, 322; Eben C. Waterman, Republican, 502.

*District No. 5.—Abington, Whitman.—*FRANKLIN P. HARLOW of Whitman, Republican, was born in Springfield, Vt., Dec. 8, 1827, and was educated in the public schools. Enlisted in Co. K, 7th regiment, June 15, 1861, and served in the Army of the Potomac; wounded at Fredericksburg; promoted to major and lieutenant-colonel; mustered out June 17, 1864. Commander of Post 78, G. A. R. Is a mechanic. Member of board of registration. Member of Puritan lodge of Masons, of Knights Templar, and of Plymouth Rock lodge of Knights of Pythias. Member of House in 1871-2-94-5, on committees on labor and library; on committee on military affairs, 1898.

Vote of district: J. T. Doten, Prohibition, 32; Franklin P. Harlow, Republican, 594; C. D. Nash, Democrat, 501.

*District No. 6.—Carver, Lakeville, Marion, Mattapoisett, Rochester, Wareham.—*NATHANIEL G. STAPLES of Lakeville, Republican, was born in Middleboro, June 1, 1851, and was educated in the public schools and Pierce Academy. Is a farmer and carpenter. Selectman and assessor in 1896-7. On committees on elections, and libraries, 1898.

Vote of district: Nathaniel G. Staples, Republican, 341 all others, 11.

*District No. 7.—Halifax, Middleborough, Plympton.—*DAVID G. PRATT, Republican, of Middleborough, was born in Boston, Nov. 7, 1848; educated in private schools and Phillips Exeter Academy, class of 1856. In mercantile business until he retired in 1886. Town electric light commissioner, 1894-5; treasurer, secretary and trustee of the Pratt Free School of North Middleborough. Member of Joseph Warren lodge of Masons, of Knights Templar, and of Middlesex club. On committee on water supply in the House of 1897; on same, and on printing, 1898.

Vote of district: David G. Pratt, Republican, 464; Z. E. Sherman, 164.

District No. 8.—Bridgewater East Bridgewater. West Bridgewater.—THOMAS M. CROCKER, Republican, of Bridgewater, was born in Barnstable, Dec. 27, 1832; educated in its public schools, Barnstable Academy, and at Paul Wing's private school in Sandwich. Was country merchant until 1884, and has been in life insurance business since then. Registrar of voters, ten years; selectman and overseer of the poor, two years; justice of the peace and bail commissioner at the present time. Member of the Knights of Honor and Odd Fellows. On committee on agriculture in House in 1897; on committees on agriculture, and public service in 1898.

Vote of district; Thomas W. Crocker, Republican, 389; L. W. Snow, Democrat, 147.

District No. 9.—Wards 3, 4 of Brockton.—EUGENE B. ESTES, Republican, was born in West Bridgewater, Dec. 7, 1850; educated in the public schools. Machine operator in shoe factory. Past commander of R. B. Grover camp Sons of Veterans; grand junior seneschal of Ancient Essenic Order of Mass.; past master workman of A. O. U. W. Clerk of committee on liquor law, and on federal relations in House of 1897; House chairman of federal relations, and clerk of liquor law, 1898.

Vote of district: Eugene B. Estes, Republican, 639; E. M. Henry, Democrat, 350.

District No. 10.—Wards 1, 2, 5 of Brockton.—CHARLES W. TILTON, Republican, was born in China, Me., April 6, 1836; educated in the public schools. Removed to Brockton at 18; 40 years in the shoe business; shoe finisher. Enlisted Aug. 20, 1862, in Co. K, 42d regiment; discharged July 30, 1863. Fletcher Webster Post, No. 13, G. A. R., chaplain, two years. Common council, 1883-4-5; alderman, 1886; inspector, 1882; registrar since 1887. In House of 1896, on committee on counties, and on special committee on redistricting the state; on prisons in 1897, and also in 1898.

JOHN J. WHIPPLE of Brockton, Republican, born in Worcester, December 31, 1847; educated in public schools. Removed to Brockton in 1866, and for some 25 years was engaged there in the drug and grocery business. In 1878 chosen selectman, and served temporarily as town clerk. In 1884 chosen alderman; in 1886-7-94-5, was mayor of the city. For several years chairman of the Republican city committee. In 1883 was appointed on staff of Gov. Robinson with rank of colonel; served as such also in 1884-5. From 1875 to 1883 member of school committee. In 1884 secretary of the Republican state central committee. From 1881 to 1884 water commissioner. An incorporator of the Brockton national and Brockton savings banks; director of the former, and was president of the latter until he resigned in 1892 to become president and a trustee of the Wildev savings bank of Boston, a position he now holds. One of the incorporators of the Brockton Agricultural society, and its treasurer for several years. In 1885 was chairman of the famous board of arbitration which settled the big strike in the Brockton shoe factories. A grand officer of Odd Fellows, Knights of Pythias, and New England Order of Protection. Member of Paul Revere lodge of Masons, of Bay State commandery of Knights Templar, of Brockton colony of Pilgrim Fathers, and of Brockton lodge of A. O. U. W. Member of the Brockton Commercial club, New England club, Elks' club, Mayors' club of

Massachusetts, and appointed on the state board of pharmacists in 1889; justice of the peace and notary public. In House of 1885, on committee on water supply (chairman), and insurance (clerk). Chairman of public charitable institutions, and on public health, 1898.

Vote of district: E. L. Brown, Democratic Citizens, 519; C. H. Coulter, Democratic Citizens, 473; Charles W. Tilton, Republican, 804; John J. Whipple, Republican, 779.

District No. 11.—Wards 6, 7 of Brockton.—DAVID WALLACE BATTLES of Brockton, Republican, was born in that city, Jan. 20, 1854; educated in the public schools and Cornell University class of 1875. Member of the Brockton school board since 1889. Trustee of the public library since 1887. In the shoe business. Past master of Paul Revere lodge of Masons, past high priest, past thrice illustrious master and past commander Bay State commandery. Member of House in 1892, chairman of committee on elections, and on committee on water supply; on committee on mercantile affairs in House of 1898.

Vote of district: David W. Battles, Republican, 610; E. E. Herrod, Democrat, 392.

SUFFOLK COUNTY.

District No. 1.—Ward 1 of Boston.—HUGH L. STALKER, Republican, was born in Nova Scotia, Dec. 31, 1859, educated in the public schools. Is a grocer. Member of common council 1893-4. Member of the Masons and Odd Fellows. On committee on metropolitan affairs in House of 1897; on committees on banks and banking, and railroads, 1898.

Vote of district: John L. Bates, Republican, 1665; J. R. Hobdell, Democrat, 642; Hugh L. Stalker, Republican, 1523; R. F. Stewart, Democrat, 635.

District No. 2.—Ward 2 of Boston.—JOHN L. KELLY, Democrat, born in Boston, March 29, 1869; public schools. Grocer. Member of Knights of Columbus, Good Fellows, and A. O. H. Common council 1895-6. Committee on mercantile affairs, 1897; clerk of same, 1898.

JAMES O'CONNOR, Democrat, born in (East) Boston, June 15, 1862; public schools. Plasterer. President of Plasterer's International association of U. S. and Can. Committee on roads and bridges, 1898.

Vote of district: F. E. Fisher, Republican, 487; E. F. Keen, Republican, 446; John L. Kelly, Democrat, 1686; James O'Connor, Democrat, 1637.

District No. 3.—Ward 3 of Boston.—T. FRANK NOONAN, Democrat, of Boston, was born in Boston (Charlestown) and was educated in the public schools, Charlestown High school. Admitted to the Massachusetts bar in 1884 in Suffolk County, and to the bar of the United States court. Member of Democratic ward committee several years, and one of the first members of Young Men's Democratic club of Massachusetts. Member of Boston bar association, Charitable Irish Society, Urbane Associates, and many other social organizations. On committee on the judiciary in House of 1898.

PETER F. TAGUE, Democrat, born in Boston, June 4, 1871; public schools. Book-keeper and N. E. representative of Neverslip Manufacturing Company. A. O. U. W. Committee on federal relations, 1897; on committee on cities, 1898.

Vote of district: E. F. Churchill, Republican, 484; T. Frank Noonan, Democrat, 1329; L. H. Schuler, Republican, 448; Peter F. Tague, Democrat, 1277.

District No. 4.—Ward 5 of Boston.—WILLIAM E. MAHONEY, Democrat, born in Boston, May 15, 1872; public schools. Rhode Island School of Design. Machinist, caterer. Common council 1895-6. Committee on constitutional amendments, 1898.

JEREMIAH J. MCCARTHY, Republican, was born in Charlestown, 1852, and was educated in Bunker Hill school. Early earning his own living, he learned the morocco-dressing trade, which he followed several years. Was a member of Washington hose company. Was first treasurer of Charlestown Volunteer Firemen's association, was originator of the Firemen's Tournament on June 17, 1890, and Gov. Brackett put him on the state board of fire commissioners to expend the $10,000 for disabled firemen; president of the Charlestown Volunteer Firemen association. Before and after Charlestown was annexed to Boston he was active in politics although this is the first office for which he has allowed his name to be used. In 1888, he was a leading spirit in the movement that sent Gen. Banks to Congress. He was alternate delegate to the Republican national convention at Minneapolis in 1892; assistant water commissioner of Boston, appointed by Mayor Curtis, at a salary of $3500, until resigning; member of Middlesex club, and of the Charlestown club. Director of Charlestown trade association. Recommended by Senators Hoar and Lodge and appointed by Gen. Horace Porter one of three persons to serve on his staff to represent Massachusetts at the inauguration of President McKinley, March 4, 1897. Inspector in the U. S. custom service from 1882 to 1893. Committees on harbors and public lands, and rapid transit in House of 1893; clerk of committee on railroads, and on committee on transit, 1894; committees on constitutional amendments and railroads, 1895. House chairman of committee on constitutional amendments, and on railroads, and member of the committee to redistrict the state, 1896; clerk of railroads, and on metropolitan affairs, 1897; monitor 1894 5-6-7-8; House chairman of committee on railroads, and on rules, 1898.

Vote of district: W. E. Mahoney, Democrat, 852; Jeremiah J. McCarthy, Republican, 1245; M. E. Smith, Republican, 818; H. L. Wightman, Democrat, 696.

District No. 5.—Ward 5 of Boston.—WILLIAM J. MILLER, Democrat, born in Boston, June 8. 1868; public schools, Boston University Law School, 1892. Lawyer. Common council four years. Committee on judiciary, 1898.

EDMUND J. TWOMEY, Democrat, was born in Boston (Charlestown), July 16, 1860; educated in the grammar schools. In the wall paper business from 1874 to 1884, and since then has been in the crockery business. On committee on drainage in House of 1898.

Vote of district: G. W. Bliss, Republican, 555, William J. Miller, Democrat, 1066; C. W. Phelps, Republican, 516; Edmund J. Twomey, Democrat, 1097.

District No. 6.—Ward 6 of Boston.—DANIEL J. KANE, Democrat, born in Boston, April 14, 1872; public schools. Committee on cities, 1898.

JOHN A. ROWAN, Democrat, born in Boston, Nov. 9, 1872; private schools. Is a cutter. Common council 1896-7. Knights of Columbus. Committee on liquor law, 1898.

Vote of district: A. De Filippo, Republican, 643; Daniel J. Kane, Democrat, 1242; F. J. Lewis, Republican Independent N. P., 100; A. Pinkofsky, Republican, 657; John A. Rowan, Democrat, 1081; J. H. Shannon, Democrat Independent, N. P., 568.

District No. 7.—Ward 7 of Boston.—WILLIAM T. A. FITZGERALD, Democrat, born in Boston, Dec. 19, 1871; English High school, Boston University Law School, 1897. Stenographer until 1897; now a lawyer. Common council, 1897. Knights of Columbus. On committee on metropolitan affairs, 1898.

THOMAS MACKEY, Democrat, was born in Watertown N. Y., Aug. 6, 1865; educated in the public schools. Is a cornice manufacturer and real estate agent. Member of common council in 1896. President of Cornice Makers' union 1885-6.

President of Manhattan literary and athletic club from 1894 to 1898; past grand arcon of the Hyptaphos; member of division 56 A. O. H.; secretary of ward 7 Democratic committee from 1896 to 1898. On committees on pay roll, and printing in House of 1898.

Vote of district: F. Arrigo, Republican Independent N. P., 17; J. H. Beloin, Citizens, 17; F. M. Brinnick, Republican, 439; J. J. Falvey, Democrat Independent N. P., 709; William T. A. Fitzgerald, Democrat, 885; S. T. Frothingham, Republican Citizens N. P., 94; W. A. Lewis, Republican Citizens N. P., 79; Thomas Mackey, Democrat, 850; J. G. Munro, Republican, 304.

District No. 8.—Ward 8, Boston.—FRANCIS J. HORGAN, Democrat, of Boston, was born in that city, July 2, 1869; educated in the public schools, and Boston College, and Boston University Law School class of 1895. Did newspaper work on Boston Globe after graduation from Boston College until taking up the study of law. Member of common council in 1896-97. District deputy supreme knight of Knights of Columbus, and member of West End council of that order. On committee on probate and insolvency in House of 1898.

DANIEL J. KILEY, Democrat, born in Boston, July 27, 1874; public schools. Paving contractor. Knights of Columbus. Common council in 1896-7. On committee on insurance in House of 1898.

Vote of district: J. F. Connor, Democrat Independent N. P., 217; H. Gediman, Republican, 754; G. W. Hill, Republican, 705; Francis J. Horgan, Democrat, 1641; Daniel J. Kiley, Democrat, 1493.

District No. 9.—Ward 9 of Boston.—JOHN J. GARTLAND, JR., Democrat, of Boston, was born in that city, Nov. 27, 1871; educated in public schools, English High school class of 1888. Is a book keeper. Member of common council, 1895. On committee on printing in House of 1898.

DAVID A. MAHONEY, Democrat, born in Boston, Dec. 21, 1867; public schools and commercial college. Book-keeper, salesman, etc. Democratic ward and city committee, 1895-6-7-8; Pastime social club; Mayonia associates. Committees on elections, and public health, 1898.

Vote of district: A. H. Farnham, Republican, 740; John J. Gartland, Jr. Democrat, 1266; F. H. Krebs, Jr., Republican Citizens, 1043; David A. Mahoney, Democrat, 1199; J. F. Ryan, Democrat Independent, N. P., 298.

District No. 10.—Ward 10 of Boston.—CHARLES S. CLERKE, Republican, was born in Falmouth, Jan. 10, 1849; educated in the public schools. Enlisted in June, 1864, in Co. A, 5th regiment, and later in 92d New York; mustered out in December, 1864. Member of Dahlgren post No. 2, G. A. R., commander of same in 1895. Wholesale tobacco and cigar business. Member of Joseph Warren lodge of Masons. On committee on metropolitan affairs in House of 1898.

CHARLES H. INNES, Republican, was born in Boston, Aug. 6, 1870; educated in the public schools and Boston University Law School, class of 1892. Is a lawyer. Member of common council in 1896. On committee on railroads in House of 1897; clerk of committee on judiciary, 1898.

Vote of district: Charles S. Clerke, Republican, 1530; Charles H. Innes, Republican, 1645; C F Richards, Democrat, 482.

District No. 11.—Ward 11 of Boston.—FRANCIS C. LOWELL, Republican, was born in Boston, Jan. 7, 1855; was educated in private schools and Harvard College, class of 1876. Is a lawyer, with offices in the Exchange building; member of firm of Lowell, Stimson & Stockton. Member of common council, 1889-90-91. In the House of 1895, on committee on rules and judiciary. House chairman of committee on ways and means, and on committees on rules and taxation, 1896; House chairman of committee on ways and means, and on committee on rules, 1897. Elected to the House of 1898 and appointed in his former committee places. Having been appointed by President McKinley as judge of the United States district court, he resigned his membership of the Legislature on January 11, and was succeeded by George S. Selfridge who was chosen at a special election, and was appointed on the committee on constitutional amendments.

CHARLES R. SAUNDERS of Boston, Republican, was born in Cambridge, November 22, 1862; educated in the public schools of Cambridge, in Harvard College, class of 1884, and the Harvard Law School, class of 1888. Is a lawyer, with office at 40 Water street, Boston. President of Harvard Union, 1883-4; member of Harvard Phi Beta Kappa, member of the Republican club of Massachusetts, 1896-7-8; chairman of committee on rules of the Boston Republican city committee, 1897; member of Boston common council, 1897, being on committees on ordinances and law department, judiciary, mayor's address and registry department. Member of the University and Middlesex clubs and of the Citizens' association. Clerk of committee on constitutional amendments in House of 1898.

Vote of district: J. E. Ansell, Democrat, 420; M. A. Fitzgerald, Democrat, 470; Francis C. Lowell, 2018; Charles R. Saunders, Republican, 1801.

District No. 12.—Ward 12 of Boston.—JOHN B. DUMOND of Boston, Republican, was born in New York, Dec. 25, 1862, and was educated in public and private schools. Is a draughtsman and mechanical engineer. Member of common council in 1897. Member Home Market club, Republican club of Massachusetts, Mercantile library association, Republican ward and city committee 1893-4-5-6-7-8, chairman in 1895-6-7. On committees on elections, and liquor laws, 1898.

ALFRED S. HAYES, Democrat, was born in Boston, May 14, 1869; graduated from Boston Latin school, 1887, from Harvard College in 1891, and from Harvard Law School in 1894. After graduating from college traveled seven months in Europe. In 1892 was on the debating team from Harvard which beat Yale. Since graduating from the Law School has practiced law in Boston. Has never been in politics before. On committee on metropolitan affairs in House of 1898.

Vote of district: John B. Dumond, Republican, 1366; Alfred S. Hayes, Independent, 1024; C. F. Morse, Republican, 963; J. H. Corcoran, 167; J. P. Walsh, 166.

District No. 13.—Ward 13 of Boston.—HUGH W. BRESNAHAN, Democrat, born in Boston Nov. 25, 1869; public schools. Sanitary engineer. Common council 1896-7. On committee on election laws, 1898.

JAMES B. CLANCY, Democrat, born in Boston, May 26, 1868; public schools. Telegrapher. Democratic city committee 1894-5-6, K. of C., and social clubs. House 1897, committee on insurance; street railways, 1898.

Vote of district: Hugh W. Bresnahan, Democrat Independent N. P., 1326; James B. Clancy, Democrat, 1326; J. T. Mahoney, Democrat, 1279; O. Peterson, Republican, 119; P. M. Peterson, Republican, 105; C. Ziemann, Democrat Independent, N. P., 107.

District No. 14.—Ward 14 of Boston.—JOHN E. BALDWIN, Democrat, born in (South) Boston, June 26, 1869; public schools, commercial college. Bookkeeper. Common council, 1894-5-6. A. O. H.; K. of C. Clerk of committee on federal relations, 1897; clerk of committee on libraries, and on prisons, 1898.

DAVID J. GLEASON, Democrat, born in (South) Boston, July 14, 1864; public schools. Machinist. Ward committee, 1897-8; Somerset and Wiskett associates. Committee on fisheries and game, 1898.

Vote of district: John E. Baldwin, Democrat, 1699; David J. Gleason, Democrat, 1515; J. J. Wall, Republican, 1108; E. O. Whitetmore, Republican, 779.

District No. 15.—Ward 15 of Boston.—WILLIAM KELLS, Jr., Democrat, born in Boston Oct. 23, 1861; public schools. Custom shirt cutter. Committees on public health, and State House, 1898.

JOHN A. MCMANUS, Democrat, was born in Bangor, Me., March 29, 1860; public schools. Iron roller, fruit dealer. Ancient Order of Hibernians, Wolftone association, and Foresters. On committee on harbors and public lands, 1897; on same committee, 1898.

Vote of district: W. Ashton, Republican, 699; C. H. G. Ferguson, Republican, 752; William Kells, Jr., 1283; John A. Mc Manus, Democrat, 1350.

District No. 16.—Ward 16 of Boston.—OSGOOD C. BLANEY, Republican, was born in Boston, Jan. 20, 1860; educated in its public schools. Is a metal refiner. Common council, 1890; sealer of weights and measures, 1895-6. Member of Odd Fellows. Committee on election laws, in House of 1897; House chairman of committee on election laws, 1898. Resigned his position in the House in March to accept a position as assistant appraiser in customs service.

ALBERT W. LYON, Republican, was born in Skowhegan, Me., March 1, 1869, educated in the public schools, Boston University Law School, class of 1893. Is a lawyer. Member of Union lodge of Masons, of Dorchester royal arch chapter, of Boston council, and of Boston commandery of Knights Templar. Is a member also of the Ancient and Honorable Artillery, the Old Dorchester club, the Boston Marketmen's club, and the League of American Wheelmen. On committees on constitutional amendments, and public service in the House of 1897; House chairman of former, and on harbors and public lands in 1898.

Vote of district: Osgood C. Blaney, Republican, 1337; T. F. Donovan, Democrat, 1005; J. Drohan, Democrat, 1124; Albert W. Lyon, Republican, 1217.

District No. 17.—Ward 17 of Boston.—RICHARD W. GARRITY, Democrat, born in Salem, March 14, 1864; public schools. Clerk 15 years; driver, motorman. A. O U. W., A. O. H., A. F. L., and various labor, political and social organizations. Committee on labor, 1898.

GEORGE H. NORTON, Democrat, was born in Boston, May 28, 1863; public schools. Real estate. Democratic ward committee. Committee on water supply; 1897: education, 1898.

Vote of district: W. Ballantyne, Republican, 942; Richard W. Garrity, Democrat, 1501; C. J. Kidney, Republican, 1222; George H. Norton, Democrat, 1277.

District No 18.—Ward 18 of Boston.—THOMAS A. CONROY, Democrat, born in Boston (Roxbury), Dec. 9, 1869; public schools. Clerk. Committee on federal relations, 1898.

MICHAEL E. GADDIS, Democrat, born in Boston, Feb. 21, 1869; public schools. Common council, 1895-6-7. Committees on libraries, and public service, 1898.

Vote of district: T. Adams, Republican, 793; E. P. Benjamin, Republican, 820; Thomas A. Conroy, 1198; Michael E. Gaddis, Democrat, 1146.

District No. 19.—Ward 19 of Boston.—JOHN J. FENENO, Democrat, born in Boston, March 24, 1866; Comins school. Salesman for Boston furnace company. On committee on liquor law, 1897; on same committee, 1898.

OLIVER S. GRANT, Democrat, born in Boston (Roxbury), April 30, 1865; public schools. Electrical contractor. Committee on education, 1897; manufactures, 1898.

Vote of district: John J. Feneno, Democrat, 1853; Oliver S. Grant, Democrat, 1779; W. Metzger, Republican, 631; R. A. Watson, Republican, 530.

District No. 20.—*Ward* 20 *of Boston.*—THOMAS COGSWELL BACHELDER, Republican, born in Gilmanton, N. H., Nov. 6, 1860; Harvard College, 1883, Harvard Law School, 1886. Common council, 1896. Royal Arcanum, clerk of Harvard improvement association, treasurer of Harvard Congregational church. Clerk of committee on probate and insolvency, and on constitutional amendments, 1897; clerk of former, and on insurance, 1898. Chickatawbut club.

JOSEPH I. STEWART, Republican, was born in Bloomfield, New Brunswick, April 25, 1847; educated in the public schools. Piano and cabinet wood work, and real estate and builder for the last 13 years. A master Mason, a chapter Mason, a Knight Templar, and supreme trustee of U. O. G. C. On committee on metropolitan affairs in House of 1897; on same committee, 1898.

Vote of district: Thomas C. Bachelder, Republican. 1792; J. J. O'Neil, Democrat, 898; W. J. Power, 831; Joseph I. Stewart, Republican, 1700.

District No. 21.—*Ward* 21 *of Boston.*—RICHARD F. ANDREWS, Jr., Republican, was born in Lynn, April 13, 1863; educated in Boston public schools. Has been in a law office; now in real estate and insurance business. Member of common council, 1893-4-5. Member of Nelson A. Miles camp No. 46, Sons of Veterans; Roxbury club, and Dudley association; of Roxbury military historical society, and of Roxbury charitable society. Committee on insurance, 1897; on same committee, 1898.

WILLIAM E. SKILLINGS, Republican, of Boston, son of the late David N. Skillings, was born in Boston, Oct. 28, 1843; educated in Winchester High school and Harvard College, class of 1866. Then spent several years in European travel, and as a war correspondent was eye-witness of the stirring events of the Franco-Prussian war, and entered Paris with the French National Guard when that city was taken from the Communists in 1871. On his return to this country he assumed the management of his father's extensive lumber interests in Maine and resided in that state for a number of years. He is a member of an English corporation extensively engaged in the lumber business, and is one of the directors and resident manager in this country. Member of the University and Roxbury clubs; and of Joseph Warren commandery of Knights Templar. On committee on manufactures in House of 1897, and author of its able and exhaustive report of the gas fatalities in Boston, a subject referred to that committee by special order of the two branches. On same committee, and clerk of committee on State House in 1898.

Vote of district: L. Abraham, Democrat, 640; Richard F. Andrews, Jr., Republican, 1762; E. Seaver, Democrat, 782; William E. Skillings, Republican, 1609.

District No. 22.—*Ward* 22 *of Boston.*—JOHN BLEILER, Republican, was born in Bavaria, Germany, May 9, 1837; public schools; removed to this country in 1850. Provision dealer. K. of H.; Pilgrim Fathers; Schwaban Verein; Kossuth lodge No. 24 D. O. H. In militia 32 years. Committee on liquor law 1897; same, 1898.

RANDOLPH V. KING of Boston, Republican, was born in Philadelphia, Jan. 20, 1853; and was educated in public and private schools, and is now studying law. Was a silk hatter for four years, a machinery painter for 12 years, and for eight years in the house and sign painting business for himself. Secretary and on executive committee of Ward 22 Republican committee in 1896; chairman of same in 1897. Past noble grand of Quinobequin lodge of Odd Fellows, past sachem of Anawan tribe of Red Men. On committee on probate and insolvency, 1898.

Vote of district: John Bleiler, Republican, 1347; J. A. Desmond, Democrat, 1035; E. C. Kelly, Democrat, 974; Randolph V. King, Republican, 1228.

District No 23.—Ward 23 of Boston.—FRANK W. ESTEY, Republican, was born in Limerick, Me., Dec. 16. 1866; educated in public schools. Is a bookkeeper. On committee on insurance in House of 1897; on committee on cities, 1898.

LEMUEL W. PETERS, Republican, born Blue Hill, Me., July 29, 1860; educated at Blue Hill Academy, Wesleyan University, class of 1884, and Boston University Law School, class of 1887; was admitted to Suffolk Bar, 1887. On committee on constitutional amendments, and State House (clerk) in House of 1897: on committee on judiciary, 1898.

Vote of district: F. O. Coughlan. Democrat, 969; Frank W. Estey, Republican, 1469; T. F. Lally, Democrat, 1094; Lemuel W. Peters, Republican, 1421.

District No. 24.—Ward 24 of Boston.—JONATHAN B. L. BARTLETT, Republican was born in Jay. Me., Oct. 11, 1849; educated in the public schools and Wilton Academy. Removed to Dorchester in 1873, and for 21 years, as superintendent, was connected with the Mattapan post office, conducting it so well that it was officially pronounced the best conducted office of its size in the country. Resigning from that position some four years ago, he has since been in the real estate business, being treasurer and manager of the Blue Hill terrace company; director of Boston Milton & Brockton street railway company. Member of Macedonia lodge of Masons, of St. Stephen chapter, of Hyde Park council and of Cyprus commandery of Knights Templar, and 32d° Mason; and member of Roxbury Military Historical Society. On committees on elections and taxation in House of 1897, also on special committee in connection with the reception of the "Bradford" manuscript; chairman of committee on elections, and on taxation, 1898.

EDWARD B. CALLENDER, Republican, was born in Boston, Feb. 23, 1851: educated in the public schools and Harvard College, class of 1872, and Harvard Law School, 1874. Is an attorney at law: also an author of "Thaddeus Stevens, Commoner: a biography", and of "The Leg Pullers, a political story." Member of the House of 1879, on committee on probate and insolvency; on same committee, and on public health, 1897: House chairman of the committee on public health, and on street railways, 1898.

Vote of district. John B. L. Bartlett, Republican, 1741; Edward B. Callender, Republican, 1765; T. J. Killian, Democrat, 740; C. F. M. Malley, Democrat, 752.

District No 25.—Ward 25 of Boston.—FREDERICK HAMMOND, Republican, was born in Ashburnham, Feb. 27, 1847; educated in public schools and Bryant & Stratton's commercial college. Enlisted Aug. 23, 1864, in Co. H, 4th Mass. Heavy Artillery, served in Va, mustered out June 17, 1865. Vice commander of post 92 G. A. R Is a merchant. On committee on harbors and public lands, 1897: on committe on cities, 1898.

LEONARD W. ROSS of Boston, Republican, was born in Worcester, Oct 5, 1856, and was educated in public and private schools. Has followed horticulture, landscape architecture and forestry. Past master and past officer of the grand lodge of Masons for Massachusetts. On committee on harbors and public lands, clerk. 1898.

Vote of district: D D. Corcoran, Democrat, 924; Frederick Hammond, Republican, 1131; Leonard W. Ross, Republican, 1065; G. H. Wentworth, Democrat, 961.

District No. 26.—Wards 1, 2 of Chelsea.—MELVIN L. BREATH, Democrat, of Chelsea was born in New Orleans, La., December 7, 1858; educated in the public schools. Is in the produce business. Member of Chelsea common council in 1889; Chelsea board of trade; and of A. O. U. W. On committees on bills in 3d reading, and public service in House of 1898.

Vote of district: F. O. Barnes, Republican, 780; Melvin L. Breath, Democrat, 931.

District No. 27.—Wards 3, 4 of Chelsea.—EDWARD E. WILLARD, Republican of Chelsea, born in Lancaster, Sept. 25, 1862; educated in Worcester Academy and Hinman's business college, Worcester. For 11 years with E. L. Rollins of Boston, wall paper manufacturer and jobber; N. E. agent for M. H. Birge & Sons of Buffalo, N. Y., wall paper manufacturers. Masons, K of P., Veteran Firemen's Association. Common council of Chelsea, 1890; aldermen, 1892-3-4. Clerk of committee on harbors and public lands, 1895; committees on harbors and public lands, and printing, 1896; mercantile affairs, 1898.

Vote of district: T. J. Morrison, Democrat, 330; Edward E. Willard, Republican, 921.

District No. 28.—Wards 5 of Chelsea, Revere, Winthrop—SCOTT F. BICKFORD, Republican, of Revere, was born in Newburyport, Nov. 14, 1864, and was educated in its public schools. From 1882 until 1883 was on the Eastern as railroad station agent, telegraph operator; was stenographer and telegraph operator from 1883 until 1891, and since then has been a stock and bond broker, senior partner of Bickford & Richards. Is a 32d degree Mason, member of Newburyport commandery Knights Templar, Massachusetts consistory, Aleppo temple Mystic Shrine; of Mystic lodge of Odd Fellows of Chelsea; of Paul Revere council of Royal Arcanum of Beachmont; Society of Colonial Wars, Sons of the American Revolution; of Mayflower commandery of the Golden Cross of Revere; of Winnisimet colony of Pilgrim Fathers of Revere; and of the Review club of Chelsea, also Middlesex club. A national bank director, also director in several corporations. For two years was president of Revere board of trade. Committee on banks and banking in House of 1897; on committee on metropolitan affairs, 1898.

Vote of district: Scott F. Bickford, Republican, 1349; O. Sullivan, Democrat, 282.

WORCESTER COUNTY.

District No. 1.—Athol, Phillipston, Royalston.—OSCAR T. BROOKS, of Athol, Republican, was born in Petersham, June 6, 1839, and was educated in public schools and New Salem Academy. Has been in mercantile business with a general store, but latterly wholly of groceries. Served as selectman, assessor, and overseer of the poor in 1881-2. Is a trustee and auditor of the Athol savings bank, and director of the Athol co-operative bank; director of board of trade; president Y. M. C. A. On committee on taxation, 1898.

Vote of district: Oscar T. Brooks, Republican Independent N P., 804; H. L. Hapgood, Republican, 623.

District No. 2.—Ashburnham, Gardner, Templeton, Winchendon.—FRANCIS LELAND of Templeton (Otter River), Republican, was born in that town, Oct. 3, 1839, and was educated in the public schools. Keeps a general store. Member of the school committee for nine years, 1872 to 1881; trustee of the public library, 1872 to 1896; trustee of the Templeton savings bank from 1875 to to 1898; trustee of the Hospital Cottages for Children from 1884 to 1898, and registrar of voters from 1888 to 1898; postmaster at Otter River from 1867 to 1885. On committee on education, 1898.

LEVI G. MCKNIGHT, Republican of Gardner, was born in Ellington, Ct., April 30. 1843; educated in the public schools. Enlisted in Co. H, 25th regiment, Sept. 17th, 1861; mustered out Jan. 26, 1865; member of Post 10, G.

A. R.; commander of Post 116 for two years: first national color bearer of the Grand Army to carry the national flag; served on Gen. Alger's staff and on Capt. "Jack" Adams' staff; past president of ex-prisoners of war association; chairman of national ex-prisoners of war association; vice-president of Massachusetts ex-prisoners of war association; vice-president of the Boys in Blue of '61 and '65. Member of A. O. U. W.; of Athlestan lodge of Masons, of North Star chapter, of Hiram council, and warden of Ivanhoe commandery of Knights Templar. Manufacturer of patent chair, wood working and sanding machinery. On committee on military affairs in House of 1897; on committees on banks and banking, and military affairs, 1898.

Vote of district: G. N. Dyer, Democrat, 896; J. W. Hutchins, Democrat, 529; Francis Leland, Republican, 1103; Levi G. McKnight, Republican, 918.

*District No. 3.—Barre, Dana, Hardwick, Hubbardston, Petersham, Westminster.—*AUSTIN F. ADAMS, of Barre Plains, Republican, was born in the town of Barre, July 15, 1840, and was educated in the Barre High school and New Salem Academy. He has been a farmer and house builder. He served as selectman in 1871-3-82-3-6-7. He is a director of the First national bank of Barre, a trustee of the Barre savings bank, a director of the town library, and president of the Worcester County West Agricultural society. On the committee on agriculture, 1898.

Vote of district: Austin F. Adams, Republican, 572; all others, 5.

*District No. 4.—Holden, New Braintree, North Brookfield, Oakham, Princeton, Rutland.—*CHARLES E. PARKER, Republican, of Holden, was born in Millbury, Oct. 20, 1833; direct line from Thomas Parker, who came over from England, March 11, 1635; also direct descendant in third generation from Capt. Timothy Parker, Jr, who led a company of "Minute Men" from Sturbrige at the battle of Lexington. Educated in Leicester, Westfield and Amherst academical schools from 1850 to 1853 Is a farmer, market gardener and florist. Member of the school committee from 1886 to the present, except one year. Assessor in 1885-6; selectman 1885-8-9-90; chairman in 1890; since its erection in 1888, trustee nearly every year of Damon Memorial and Gale Free Library; justice of peace seven years; re-appointed last year for second term. Member of Sons of American Revolution. On committee on agriculture in House of 1898.

Vote of district: Charles E. Parker, Republican, 565; all others, 2.

*District No. 5.—Brookfield, Sturbridge, Warren, West Brookfield.—*HENRY V. CROSBY of Brookfield, Republican, was born in that town, Feb. 27, 1832, and was educated in the public and private schools of his native town. Is a merchant. Town clerk, ten years; treasurer and collector, 26; selectman, 1; trustee and treasurer of the Merrick public library, 15. On committees on elections, and libraries, 1898.

Vote of district: Henry V. Crosby, Republican, 596; J. F. Hill, Democrat, 242.

*District No. 6.—Leicester, Paxton, Spencer.—*JEROME BOTTOMLY of Leicester, Republican, was born in that town (Cherry Valley), Aug. 14, 1842, and was educated in the public schools and Leicester Academy. Enlisted in Co. C, United States Engineers, Sept. 24, 1861, and served in the Army of the Potomac; promoted to be artificer, and was mustered out Sept. 24, 1864. Member of George H. Thomas post 131 of Leicester, and has been commander two years, now being quartermaster. Kept a general merchandise store 32 years; postmaster, 1868-72; selectman, 1889-90; also on board of health and overseer of the poor, 1889 90, chairman of board in 1890. On committee on drainage, 1898.

Vote of district: Jerome Bottomly, Republican, 686; George Whitford, Democrat, 390.

District No. 7.—Charlton, Dudley, Oxford, Southbridge, Webster.—ALBERT F. HISCOX of Dudley, Republican, was born in Brimfield, May 9, 1852, and was educated in the public schools and Nichols Academy. Has followed the farming and stone business. Overseer of Dudley Grange. On committee on agriculture, 1898.

ANDREW R. SNOW of Webster, Republican, was born in Tolland Conn., May 5, 1844, and was educated in the public schools. Enlisted Aug. 25, 1862, in Co. G, 51st regiment, and served in the Department of North Carolina; mustered out July 27, 1863, as corporal. Commander of Nathaniel Lyon post 61, G. A. R., for seven years, and still a member. Was a mason from 1866 to 1873, and has been a farmer since then. Assessor, 1884-5; selectman, 1890-96, inclusive; superintendent of highways from 1890 to the present. Member of Manenexet lodge of Odd Fellows; of Dudley Grange, and of Phoenix council of Royal Arcanum. On committee on prisons, 1898.

Vote of district: Albert F. Hiscox, Republican, 1070; T. Reilley, Democrat, 750; Andrew R. Snow, Republican, 1289; J. A. Whittaker, Democrat, 939.

District No. 8.—Auburn, Douglas, Millbury, Sutton.—THOMAS H. MEEK of East Douglas, Republican, was born in Fishkill, N. Y., Jan. 30, 1840, and was educated in public and private schools. In mercantile business, (cashier and superintendent of Douglas Axe Manufacturing company and of American Axe and Tool company from 1865 until 1897). Selectman and town clerk, 1878 to 1889. Member of A. O. U. W., now past master workman of East Douglass lodge, and district deputy grand master workman. Member of House in 1871. On committee on towns, 1898.

Vote of district: J. W. Brigham, Democrat, 224; Thomas H. Meek, Republican, 523.

District No. 9.—Blackstone, Grafton, Northbridge, Shrewsbury, Uxbridge.—ROMEO E. ALLEN, Republican, of Shrewsbury, was born in that town, Oct 17, 1852, educated in the public schools. Is a civil engineer. Member of board of selectmen, 1885-6; town auditor the last nine years; chairman of Republican town committee, 1897-8. Member of the local lodge, No, 102, of Odd Fellows, and of the local grange, Patrons of Husbandry. Member of the House in 1895, serving on the committee on roads and bridges; clerk of same committee, 1898.

ARTHUR R. TAFT, of Uxbridge, Republican, was born in that town, Feb, 19, 1859, and was educated in the public schools and Mowry & Goff's Business College class of 1878. Has been in the mercantile and real estate business in Uxbridge and Boston, and is also a farmer. Selectman, 1893-96; life trustee of the public library; director of the Uxbridge National bank since 1892, and on finance committee of Uxbridge savings bank since 1891. On committee on towns, 1898.

Vote of district: Romeo E. Allen, Republican, 943; A. Elliott, Democrat, 409; A. E. Seagrave, Democrat, 435; Arthur R. Taft, Republican, 906.

District No. 10.—Hopedale, Mendon, Milford, Upton, Westborough.—WALTER S. V. COOKE, Republican, of Milford, was born there, Aug. 12, 1851; educated in public and private schools. Been in shoe business 20 years; last 13 years secretary and treasurer of the Milford co-operative bank. Past grand of Tisquantum lodge of Odd Fellows; past chief patriarch of Quinshepaug encampment of I. O. O. F.; member of Montgomery lodge of Masons, Mt Lebanon chapter of R. A. M., Milford commandery of K. T., and Aleppo Temple of Mystic Shrine. Ex-president and for the last ten years secretary of the Quidnunc association, the leading social club of Milford. Assessor, 1887; registrar from 1889 to 1896; from 1888 to 1893, secretary of the Republican town committee; 1893-4, chairman of same. House chairman of committee on towns, 1896; House chairman of towns, and on street railways, 1897; same positions, 1898.

APPLETON PARK WILLIAMS of West Upton, Republican, was born in Providence, R. I., Jan. 28, 1867; educated in Brown University class of 1889. With the Rhode Island Hospital Trust company of Providence until 1892; treasurer of the Upton Manufacturing company from 1892 till now. On Upton school committee, 1895-8, and its chairman the last two years. On committee on education, 1898.

Vote of district: Walter S. V. Cooke, Republican, 1493; J. B. Fitch, Democrat, 732; W. J. Welch, Democrat, 893; Appleton P. Williams, Republican, 1374.

District No. 11.—Berlin, Boylston, Clinton, Northboro, Southboro, Sterling, West Boylston.—ASA B. FAY of Northboro, Republican, was born in that town, Aug. 31, 1838, and was educated in its public schools. Enlisted in Co. C, 34th regiment, July 25, 1862, serving in Virginia; wounded once; promoted to lieutenant; mustered out June 16, 1865. Member Joe Johnson post 96, G. A. R., being its commander and officer of the day. Farmer, wood and lumber dealer; postmaster, three years. Assessor, 1867-8; selectman, 1870-87-8-97. Member of New Hampshire House of Representatives, 1876-7 serving on the committee on asylums for the insane, and fisheries. On committee on fisheries, 1898.

WALTER F. HOWARD, Republican, of Clinton was born in that town, Sept. 20, 1855; educated in the public schools and Bryant & Stratton's commercial college of Boston. Is in the livery and sale stable business. Chairman of road commissioners in 1895, and chief of the board of fire engineers; clerk of the Clinton & Lancaster driving park company. Member of Trinity lodge of Masons, and of Wattoquottoc tribe of Red Men. Clerk of committee on counties, and on special committee on redistricting the state, 1896; on counties, 1897; on committee on water supply, 1898.

Vote of district: Asa B. Fay, Republican, 1509; Walter F. Howard, Republican, 1596; all others, 35.

District No. 12.—Bolton, Ward 6 of Fitchburg, Harvard, Lancaster, Lunenburg.—HAROLD PARKER, Republican, of Lancaster was born in Charlestown (Boston), June 17, 1854; educated in public and private schools, Phillips Academy of Exeter, and Harvard College, class of 1875. Is in general civil engineering business, and is connected with the construction and administration of railroads. Has held various town offices from 1886 to the present time. On committee on street railways, 1898.

Vote of district: N. J. Cadorette, Democrat, 197; Harold Parker, Republican, 582.

District No. 13.—Wards 1, 2, 3, 4, 5 of Fitchburg.—ALBERT H. BURGESS of Fitchburg, Republican, was born in Grafton, Vt., May 19, 1843, and was educated in the public schools. Enlisted in Co. H, 2d United States Sharp Shooters, Oct. 16, 1861, and served in Virginia; promoted to corporal and sergeant; mustered out Feb. 16, 1863. Member of E. V. Sumner post 19 G. A. R. Is in the drug business for the past 20 years in Fitchburg. Represented his native town in the Vermont Legislature in 1874-5. Member of Fitchburg common council 1891-3-4-5, being its president the last three years; chairman of water commissioners and chairman of Republican city committee. Held various town offices in his native town. Member of Aurora lodge, Thomas chapter and Jerusalem commandery of Masons; and of Nashua tribe of Red Men. On committee on cities, 1898.

FRANCIS F. FARRAR, Republican, of Fitchburg was born in Concord, Jan. 10, 1833; educated in the public schools. Enlisted, Aug. 23, 1862, in Co. A, 53d regiment. served in division of Maj. Gen. N. P. Banks; wounded in left arm at Port Hudson, La; mustered out, Sept. 2, 1863. Is a member of E. V. Sumner post 19 G. A. R. of Fitchburg. Is a carpenter and builder. Member of common council in 1873. Member of Aurora lodge of Masons, and of Jerusalem commandery of Knights Templar. On committee on federal relations in House of 1897; on committees on ways and means, and federal relations, 1898.

Vote of district: J. W. Abbott, Democrat, 641; Albert H. Burgess, Republican, 1382; Francis F. Farrar, Republican, 1292; J. Heagney, Democrat, 563.

District No. 14.—Leominster.—ALEXANDER S. PATON of Leominster, Republican, was born in Dunbarton, Scotland, Nov. 20, 1854; educated in the public schools. Is a manufacturer of horn goods. Selectman 1891-2-3, chairman 1893. Moderator frequently of town meetings. Member of Wilder lodge of Masons, and Jerusalem commandery of Knights Templar; has passed all the chairs in Leominster lodge of Odd Fellows, and Wachusett tribe of Red Men; also member Columbia lodge of Knights of Pythias, and of Prosperity lodge of Daughters of Rebekah. Member of Republican club of Massachusetts, and of Home Market club, and is official correspondent of American Protective Tariff League. Also president of Worcester & Clinton street railway, and a director in Greenfield & Turners Falls, Gardner, and Leominster & Clinton street railway companies. On committee on ways and means, 1898.

Vote of district: H. Cook, Republican Independent N. P., 552; F. H. Mowe, Democrat, 149; Alexander S. Paton, Republican, 619.

District No. 15.—Ward 1 of Worcester.—GEORGE MAURY RICE, Republican, was born in that city, Oct. 20, 1843; educated in the public schools. Has been an inventor, photographer and manufacturer, but has retired from business. Was an army photographer during the latter part of the Rebellion, but was not enlisted. Member of common council, 1891-5, inclusive; served continuously on the committee on water and various minor committees; elected yearly by city council in joint convention, a member of the board of trustees of the City Hospital for the years 1892-5, inclusive. Member of Montacute lodge of Masons and was its master in 1884-5; grand steward in the grand lodge of Massachusetts, 1896; Worcester chapter R. A. M., and was its M. E. H. P. in 1879 80; was R. E. grand king in grand chapter, 1889, and was a delegate to the session of the general grand chapter of the United States held at Atlanta in 1889; member of Massachusetts convention of high priests, of Hiram council R. & S. M, and was its T. I. M. in 1882-3; grand P. C W. in grand council, 1884; Worcester county commandery R. T., held minor offices. Worcester lodge of Perfection 14th degree; Goddard council P. J. 16th degree, M. E. S. P. G. in 1887; Lawrence chapter Rose Croix 18th degree; Massachusetts Consistory 32d degree; 1st lieut. commander, Massachusetts Council of Deliberation, 1886; of Aleppo Temple A. A. O. N. Mystic Shrine. Member of Worcester county mechanics' association, and served three years on its board of trustees; of Worcester board of trade, of the Worcester agricultural society, and of the New England agricultural society; of Worcester society of antiquity; and of Society of Sons of American Revolution; of Worcester Continentals, capt. of Co. C; Veteran of Worcester City Guards (Co. A 2d regiment) On committee on water supply in House of 1896; clerk of water supply, 1897; House chairman of same committee, and on military affairs, 1898.

Vote of district: George M. Rice, 659; C. H. Writer, Democrat, 208.

District No. 16.—Ward 2 of Worcester.—MOSES DUDLEY GILMAN, Republican, was born in Broome, P. Q., May 23, 1846; educated in the public schools. Is a manufacturer of confectionery. Enlisted in Co M. 3d Massachusetts

Cavalry, Dec. 30, 1864, serving under Gen. Sheridan; mustered out Sept. 28, 1865. Member of George H. Ward post No. 10, G. A. R. Member of common council 1882-6, and of aldermen 1894-6. Member of the Athlestan lodge, Eureka chapter royal arch Masons; of Worcester county commandery of Knights Templar; of Lawrence chapter, Rose Croix and the Massachusetts consistory 32d degree Masons; of Regulus lodge Knights of Pythias. Member of committee on cities in the House of 1897; on same committee, 1898.

Vote of district: Moses D. Gilman, Republican Independent, N. P., 938; C. W. Wood, Republican, 596.

District No. 17.—Ward 3 of Worcester.—WILLIAM I. MCLOUGHLIN, Democrat, born in Worcester, Jan. 16, 1872; public schools, Holy Cross College, Georgetown University Law School. Lawyer; teacher. A. O. H. On committees on constitutional amendments, and probate and insolvency, 1898.

Vote of district: H. De Fosse, Republican, 321; William I. McLoughlin, Democrat, 779.

District No. 18.—Ward 4 of Worcester.—MICHAEL L. RUSSELL, Democrat, was born in Chicago, Ill., Dec. 15, 1860, and was educated in the Worcester High school. A machinist, but for the last seven years a type-writer and stenographer. Member of common council in 1889-90-1-2. On committee on drainage in House of 1897; on public charitable institutions in 1898.

Vote of district: S. S. Mackin, Republican, 62; J. H. Mellen, Democrat, 783; Michael L. Russell, Independent, 810.

District No. 19.—Ward 5 of Worcester.—JAMES F. CARBERRY, Democrat, born in Worcester, Sept. 18, 1868; public schools. Machinist; provision dealer. Democratic city committee; common council 1896; Foresters. Committee on public service, 1898.

Vote of district: James F. Carberry, Democrat, 827; A. E. Enberg, Republican, 630.

District No. 20.—Ward 6 of Worcester.—GEORGE W. COOMBS, Republican, was born in Sherborn, Nov. 4, 1837; educated in the public schools. Has been a machinist, woolen manufacturer and a wool merchant. Was an alderman from Ward 6 in Worcester for 1892-3-4-5. On committees on libraries, and State House of 1897; House chairman of committee on libraries, and on public service, 1898.

Vote of district: George W. Coombs, Republican, 721; A. W. Rose, Democrat, 185.

District No. 21.—Ward 7 of Worcester.—CHARLES R. JOHNSON of Worcester, Republican, was born in Dana, Dec. 28, 1852; educated in Worcester High school, and Harvard College class of 1875. Is a lawyer. Member of Worcester school committee, 1877-8-92-3-4-6-7-8. Master in chancery since 1882. Member of various fraternal orders. Life member of Worcester Society of Antiquity, corresponding member of Western Reserve Historical Society, author of various articles on historical subjects. On committee on probate and insolvency in House of 1898.

Vote of district: E. W. Earle, Democrat, 170; Charles R. Johnson, Republican, 656.

District No. 22.—Ward 8 of Worcester.—CHARLES G. WASHBURN, Republican, lawyer and manufacturer, was born in Worcester, Jan. 28, 1857; educated at public schools, graduated at Worcester Polytechnic Institute, 1875, at Harvard University, 1880. Admitted to Suffolk bar, 1887; was for several years a director and executive officer of the Washburn & Moen manufacturing company of Worcester. On committee on mercantile affairs in House of 1897; House chairman of committee on taxation, 1898.

Vote of district: D. D. Morgan, Democrat, 108; Charles G Washburn, Republican, 861.

THE CHAPLAIN AND CLERKS.

DANIEL WINGATE WALDRON, the chaplain of the House, was born in Augusta, Me., Nov. 11, 1840. Graduated from Bowdoin College in 1862 and from Andover Theological Seminary in 1866. Ordained and installed pastor of the Congregational church, East Weymouth, Mass., April 3, 1867; dismissed May 14, 1871, to become pastor of the Maverick church, East Boston, which position he held until Dec. 1, 1872. Since Feb 1873, connected with the City Missionary Society, Boston, being now its secretary and superintendent. Elected chaplain of the House in 1879, and re-elected each year since. Preached the "Election Sermon", Jan. 7, 1880.

JAMES W. KIMBALL, clerk, Republican, was born in Lynn, Dec. 17, 1858. He received his education in the public schools; and on leaving school he entered the printing business, which trade he has since followed In 1883 he was appointed a page of the House of Representatives, afterwards appointed a messenger of the same branch, and in 1888, when a vacancy occurred in the assistant clerkship of the House, he was appointed to fill that position. Nominated for clerk by House Republicans in caucus and elected by full House of 1897.

FRANK E. BRIDGMAN, assistant clerk, was born in Springfield, March 28, 1869. Now resides at Jamaica Plain, Boston. Graduated from High school of Toledo, O., being salutatorian of class of 1887. Entered business life Aug. 8, 1887, with Mechanics' Iron Foundry Co. of Roxbury, in whose employ he remained until appointed clerical assistant to the clerk of the Senate, Jan 1, 1894. After serving in the last-named position during three sessions of the Legislature, he was appointed assistant clerk of the House, Jan. 6, 1897.

SERGEANT-AT-ARMS AND SOME APPOINTEES.

CAPT. JOHN G. B. ADAMS, sergeant-at-arms, born in Groveland, Oct. 6, 1841. April 19, 1861 enlisted in Major Ben Perley Poore's Rifle Battalion, later part of Nineteenth regiment. Left with regiment Aug. 28, 1861, sixth corporal of Co. A; first sergeant, March 1, 1862; soon captain, which rank he held until close of war. Was in every battle of Army of the Potomac in which his regiment took part; twice saved regimental colors at Fredericksburg; twice severely wounded at Gettysburg; rejoined his regiment so as to be with it from the Wilderness to Petersburg, being captured at latter June 22, 1864; nine months in Libby. Macon, Charleston, Columbia, and Raleigh, being one of 600 kept under fire at Charleston; escaped twice; recaptured each time. Since the war, foreman in a Lynn shoe factory, inspector in Boston Custom House for 15 months, postmaster at Lynn eight years, deputy warden of the Concord reformatory one year, resigning; sergeant-at-arms, January 1886, and ever since. Past commander-in-chief of the Grand Army of the Republic; first recruit of post 5, G. A. R of Lynn; its commander three times; department commander of state one year; 19 times delegate to National encampment; many years president of Association of Survivors of Rebel Prisons. President of board of trustees of Soldiers' Home at Chelsea for 16 years. Messenger to carry the electoral vote of state to Washington in 1868.

MAJOR CHARLES G DAVIS, first clerk, born in New York city, Nov. 29, 1859; public schools. Enlisted Sept. 4, 1861, Co. C, cavalry; 1st sergt, 2d lieut, 1st lieut, captain, major. Wounded at Kelly's Ford, Va.; wounded and captured at Aldie, Va. Prisoner at Libby Prison, Danville, Macon, Charleston, Columbia, escaping from latter Nov. 4, 1864; mustered out as major. Has been secretary, vice-president and president of several organizations of veterans; Loyal

Legion; post 15, G. A. R., its commander in 1871; adjutant of Ancient and Honorable Artillery in 1875, and 1st lieut in 1887.

DAVID T. REMINGTON, of Northampton, Senate door-keeper, was born at Plainfield, June 5, 1846; educated in common schools. Enlisted Oct. 9, 1861, in Co. B, 31st Mass; discharged Oct. 23, 1865, with rank of corporal. Severely wounded at Sabine Cross Roads, La., April 8, 1864; wounded again at Blakely, near Mobile, April 8, 1865. Held all offices of Jerusalem lodge of Masons, of Northampton; deputy of the 13th Masonic district, 1891-4; W. L. Baker post G. A. R., and all its offices but commander. Appointed messenger, 1890; door-keeper, 1892.

THOMAS J. TUCKER, House door-keeper, was born in Boston, Dec. 21, 1831; graduated from the Mayhew school; engaged in business until anppointed on the messenger corps of the Legislature under Sergeant-at-arms Benjamin Stevens; appointed assistant door-keeper in 1869, and door-keeper in 1875. Mr. Tucker has been prominent in temperance work, having served in all the honorary offices of the Sons of Temperance of Massachu-etts, and was grand worthy patriarch, 1874-5; also member of the National division and life director of the Massachusetts Total Abstinence Society.

JOHN KINNEAR, assistant door-keeper, born in Glasgow, Scotland, Nov. 24, 1836, came to this country when 22 months old; lived in Cambridge ever since. Commissioned as 3d lieut. Co. C, 2d regiment, first volunteer company of the Rebellion, but on arriving at Fortress Monroe received a commission as first sergeant. At expiration of his time July 25, 1861, was discharged; then recruited Co. E, 30th regiment, and was appointed 1st lieut. by special order from President Lincoln, Jan. 19, 1862; mustered out of service, Sept. 22, 1862. Was appointed messenger of the House in 1880, and made assistant door-keeper in 1884.

CHARLES A. LEGG, chief engineer, born in Dover, N. H., Nov. 11, 1848; educated in public schools of Lowell. Apprenticeship in Lowell machine shops, finished trade at McKay & Alden's locomotive works, East Boston; some years for Merrimack manufacturing company of Lowell; for various railroads in mechanical departments, and for fourteen years had charge of mechanical department of Harvard University before taking his present place, at opening of State House Extension. Member of National association of stationary engineers. Member of Montacute lodge of Masons of Worcester.

CHARLES W. PHILBRICK of Lowell, was born in that city in 1843. Enlisted in Co. F, 3d N. H. regiment, Aug. 9, 1861; wounded at Drury Bluff May 15, 1864, and his left arm was amputated on the field; discharged in Sept., 1864. Appointed special messenger in 1872, and in August, 1892, was made regular messenger.

JAMES BEATTY, postmaster, born in Manchester, England, Aug. 26. 1845 came to this country when only two years old, going at once to Salem; educated in common schools. Enlisted Sept. 22, 1861, in Co. I, 22d Massachusetts; three yea s as bugler in Fifth Corps of Army of the Potomac, taking part in all engagements. Mustered out Oct. 18, 1864. Auctioneer and furniture business in Waltham. Alderman, 1867-8. Appointed messenger at the State House in 1886; appointed legislative post-master, 1893. Waltham G. A. R. post; Prospect lodge of Odd Fellows; A. O. U. W.

EZRA T. POPE of Sandwich, was born in that town, Aug. 27, 1825, educated in public and private schools. Is a farmer. Member of the House from First Barnstable District in 1864-65. Been constable and deputy sheriff; appointed messenger in 1874.

HENRY W. SYKES of Pittsfield, was born in Sheffield, Jan. 12, 1839; educated in the public schools. Enlisted Aug. 4, 1862, in Co. C, 37th regiment; lost right arm at Cold Harbor, Va., June 3, 1864 discharged June 17, 1865; post; 196 G. A. R. Appointed messenger 1884

EDWIN C. GOULD, of Melrose, was born Aug. 19, 1845, at Wilmington educated in Bath, Me., schools. In 1856, printed in Melrose its first paper, the Melrose Advertiser, now Melrose Journal; went to Atchison, Kan., 1857; crossed the plains in 1860 at time of Pike's Peak Gold fever, and was employed in the mines when the war broke our. Enlisted Sept. 1, 1861, in Co. F, 1st Colorado cavalry, wounded at battle of Glorietta, N. M.; discharged Oct. 16, 1864; postmaster at military post, Fort Lyon, Col., 1862 to 1865; in 1866, entered employ of Bridgeport, Conn. Rubber Company, where he remained 13 years. From 1879 to 1891, cashier for F. M. Holmes Furniture Co of Boston. Been commander of the U. S. Grant post No. 4, G. A. R.; member of "Sons of the American Revolution"; tyler of Wyoming lodge of Masons; town auditor, justice of peace, and notary public. Appointed messenger in 1891.

LOUIS AGASSIZ PHILLITS, messenger in charge of legislative document room, was born in Deerfield, Aug. 14, 1870; educated in the public schools. Appointed in sergeant-at-arms department, Jan. 1, 1894, promoted to present position, June 15, 1897. Member of Sons of American Revolution.

J. HENRY LOCKE, of Worcester, was born in Boylston, Dec. 17, 1842; educated in the public schools. Enlisted Sept. 27, 1861, in Co. D, 25th regiment, army of the Potomac and army of the James; wounded June 30, 1864; mustered out July 13, 1865; past officer of the guard of post 10 G A. R, Worcester; has been a janitor; appointed messenger of Senate, Jan., 1897.

FRANCIS A. IRELAND of Pittsfield, was born in Dexter, Me., July 27, 1843; educated in the public schools. Overseer 20 years in a woolen mill Private in Co. E, 22d Maine regiment. Past commander in G A. R.; past warden in N. E. O. P.; aide-de camp to Commander-in-chief J P. S. Gobin of G A R. Appointed Senate messenger, Jan., 1898.

ALBRO G. BEAN of Everett, was born in Bethlehem, N. H., May 29, 1838; educated in public schools. Enlisted Aug. 6, 1862, Co. G. 1st H. A. 11th Vt. Vol. promoted to Qm. sergt., mustered out July, 1865. Member James A. Perkins post G. A. R.; N. E. O. P., representative to supreme lodge four years. Printer (foreman) Appointed as messenger, Jan. 1, 1898.

SIDNEY HOLMES of Boston (South) was born in Plymouth, Aug. 21, 1843; educated in the public schools. Is a cabinet maker. Member Tremont lodge of Odd Fellows, past noble grand and past chief patriarch. Appointed House messenger, Jan. 1898, especially assigned to the Speaker's room.

C. J. TARBELL of Springfield, was born at Mt. Holly, Vt., Nov. 11, 1842; educated in the public schools. Enlisted Sept. 1, 1862, in Co. E, 16th Vermont, wounded at Gettysburg, mustered out Aug. 10, 1863; re-enlisted Jan. 30, 1865, in 26th New York cavalry; mustered out June 27, 1865, at close of the war. Cabinet maker and furniture business. Member Roswell Lee lodge and Morning Star chapter of Masons; also of Odd Fellows. Appointed House messenger, Jan. 1, 1898.

ROBERT J. TAYLOR, in charge of the elevator on the west side next the Mount Vernon street entrance, was born in Virginia in 1852, and was educated in the Hampton school. Came to Boston in 1872, and followed the hotel business until 1886, when he was appointed to position of legislative elevator man in the o d State House. A prominent member of the G. U. O. of O. F., past officer of Sumner lodge, past grand master of council of same order. and past officer of the military order. Represented his lodge in the B. M. C. held in Washington in 1892, and is a trustee of the Odd Fellows Building Association.

HARRY W. MORGAN, Senate, born in Northampton (Florence), Sept. 24, 1879; educated in public schools, including High school, also Hinman's Business College of Springfield. Appointed Senate page, Jan. 1, 1896.

LAWRENCE G. MITCHELL, Dorchester, was born in Boston, Jan. 24, 1880; educated in public schools, including High school. Appointed Senate page, Jan. 1897.

CLARENCE J. SMITH, page to the Speaker, was born in Boston, educated in the public schools, graduating from the English High School in 1893. Appointed page in 1895.

EDWARD S. BACKMAN, of Malden, was born in Bridgeport, Ct., Oct. 22, 1878; educated in the public schools. Appointed page, Jan. 1, 1896.

GEORGE W. FILLEBROWN, appointed special messenger in the sergeant-at-arms' department, was born in Mt. Vernon, Me.

NOTES OF THE SESSION.

Out of 40 Senators, 11 have "William" as their first name, and then there was Senator Williams besides.

On April 12, the Senate and House joined in a banquet at the Hotel Vendome, Governor Wolcott being their guest.

On May 25 all the senators found their desks adorned with handsome small American flags, the gift of Senator Holden.

On June 14, the Legislature made a trip down the harbor as guests of the city of Boston, to inspect the fortications, etc.

Senators Morse and Irwin and Representatives Stone, Dubuque, Attwill, Magenis and Peters were appointed a special committee to request the Governor to remove John H. Tyler from the office of justice of the peace in Boston.

Resolutions upon the death of Hon. E. A. Morse of Canton were offered in the House, June 9, by Representative Bartlett of Boston, and unanimously adopted. Similar action was taken in the Senate, June 20, Senator Roe of Worcester speaking to the resolutions.

On Tuesday, June 7, the Legislature made its second annual pilgrimmage through the Merrimack valley, on invitation of Senator George of Haverhill and Representative Hoyt of the same city. It was made by special train to Haverhill and by steamer down the Merrimack.

On March 30, Senators Morse, Soule and Moran and Representatives Clarke, Hall of Dennis, Holton. Denham, Waterman, Francis, Codman and Sears were appointed a special committee to attend the funeral of John Simpkins, late representative in Congress from the 13th Mass. district.

Senators Morse, Harwood, Leach and Moran and Representatives Myers, Kenefick, Washburn, Whipple, Dubuque, Noonan, Hall of Dennis, Trow, Keith, and Clerke were appointed to represent the General Court at the dedication of the statue of Gen. Charles Devens on the State House grounds.

Representative George S. Selfridge of the 11th Suffolk district made but a brief stay in the House. He was sworn in on March 9, having been chosen to succeed Mr. Francis C. Lowell, who had been made a United States judge. But he was shortly called to join his company, and was stationed on the "Catskill" at Gloucester. Mr. Selfridge comes of fighting ancestry, his father and grand-father being retired admirals in the United States navy on the retired list. He is a lawyer, member of the firm of Strout & Selfridge.

Senator James E. Hayes died on Feb. 8, and on March 29 David B. Shaw was chosen in his place to represent the second Suffolk district. The Senate attended his funeral in a body, Feb. 9, and Representatives Ponce, McCarthy, Porter, Hayes of Lowell, Magenis, Feneno, Twomey and Noonan were appointed a special committee to attend his funeral.

The sudden death of Senator Hayes near the beginning of the session, made necessary the immediate filling of his position on the committee on metropolitan affairs, and President Smith appointed Senator Rourke of the Third Suffolk to fill that vacancy. Senator Shaw, chosen later by the district, was then appointed to his positions on libraries and the liquor law.

Senators Parsons, Fairbank, Rourke, Irwin, Putnam, Farley and Bailey, and Representatives Estes, Farrar, Slocum, Philbrick, Swift, Drake, Bridgeo, Conroy, Clarke, McCarthy, Stone, Cooke, Ponce, Gove, Smith, Hayes of Boston, Anthony, and How (the first three senators and the first eight representatives being the committee on federal relations), were appointed a committee to represent the state at the Trans-Mississippi Exposition at Omaha.

Just at the close of the session the new "Beacon monument" was placed in position near the east entrance of the Capitol, and substantially on the same site as the famous one of the days before the Revolution, the first beacon having been erected there in 1634. The British took it down when they occupied Boston, and it was rebuilt on their evacuation only to be blown down in 1789. A new one was erected and remained until 1811, when the hill was cut down. The bronze historical tablets were removed to Doric Hall in the State House, but are now inserted in the walls of the new monument.

The committee on military affairs (Senators Brigham, Woodward and Bouve, and Representatives Marden, Mayo, McKnight, Campbell, Harlow, Richardson, Rice and Ames) and Senators Barber, Black, Hodgkins, Roe, Soule, George, Quirk, Flint and Chamberlain and Representatives Rowell, Boutwell, Fuller, Hayes of Lowell, Parsons, Crawford, Gilman, Wentworth, Howe, Crosby of Attleboro, Bottomly, White, Fitzgerald, Ramsdell, Balcom, Dalton, Boynton, Hammond, Whitcomb of Acton, Tilton, Burgess and Snow were appointed to represent the state at the dedication of the the monument erected by the Commonwealth on the battle-field of Antietam.

The Spanish-American war brought new features into the records of legislation. On May 17 Representative Butler Ames of Lawrence was given leave of absence for the remainder of the session so as to be with his regiment, the Sixth, On May 26 the House took a recess to greet Representative Joubert of Lawrence, captain of Co. F, 9th regiment, U. S. V., who had come from camp at Framingham. On April 15, Gov. Wolcott sent in a special message asking an appropriation of $500,000 for war purposes. Inside of 26 minutes a bill appropriating that sum had been passed all the stages and sent to the Governor and been signed by him. The vote in both branches was unanimous, without a word of debate, and greeted with three cheers in the Senate. There was also an appropriation made for the purchase and equipment of a hospital ship for our soldiers in service of the United States.

CORRECTION.

On page 121, Fourth Worcester Senatorial district read WILSON H. FAIRBANK in place of "William H."; on page 129, read WILLIAM S. SWIFT for "William A."

MASSACHUSETTS LEGISLATORS, 1898.

HOW THEY SIGN THEIR NAMES.

REDUCED FAC SIMILES OF THE AUTOGRAPHS OF

MASSACHUSETTS LEGISLATORS.

THE EXECUTIVE DEPARTMENT.

(PRESIDENT OF SENATE.) (SPEAKER OF HOUSE.)

THE SENATE.

MASSACHUSETTS LEGISLATORS, 1898.

THE HOUSE OF REPRESENTATIVES.

[Page of signatures of members of the Massachusetts House of Representatives, 1898. Signatures are largely illegible but appear to include names such as: Austin F. Adams, J. A. Allen, Julius C. Anthony, Thomas C. Brelsten, Frank W. Barnard, David W. Battles, Geo. E. Bemis, Horatio Bisbee, Henry M. Bosworth, Warren Boynton, William Budger, Wm. J. Bullock, A. Campbell, L. B. Chandler, Albert Clarke, N. S. Y. Locke, H. Crosby, William Cutter, Philo M. Allen, Butler Ames, Albert S. Apsey, Geo. Bolton, Geo. H. Puttitt, E. O. Beede, Frank O. Bennett, Melvin T. Brush, Geo. T. Brooks, A. H. Bergen, James F. Carberry, W. D. Chapple, John W. Connelly, Daniel S. Coolidge, Thos. W. Crocker, J. Frank Dalton, Henry C. Atkins, John E. Baldwin, Henry A. Belcher, Scott F. Bisbee, John Bliss, H. L. Bardwell, Hugh McBernahan, Charles C. Bown, E. Hallender, Jas. A. Cleary, Thomas A. Emery, A. R. Crosby, Richard E. Moore, Daniel H. Davis.]

M. D. Jones, M. B. Jones, Wm. A. Joselyn,
Joseph H. Jenkins, Daniel J. Kane, Chas. F. Keith,
William Kelley Jr., John L. Kelly, Thomas H. Kennefick,
Daniel J. Kiley, A. D. King, Randolph V. Tking,
Wm. F. Kyle, Wm. A. Lang, A. S. Lovejoy,
Francis Leland, Edw. J. Lewis, John F. Libby,
Alexander Lockhart, Francis C. Lowell, Daniel W. Lyons,
L. J. Mracken, Thomas Mackey, John E. Maguire,
David A. Mahony, William E. Mahony, William H. Marden,
B. W. Mays, Jeremiah J. O'Leary, L. B. McKnight,
William J. McLaughlin, John A. McManus, Geo. F. Mead,
J. F. Meek, George W. Mellen, William F. Miller,
Charles Terry Mills, James A. Montgomery, Andrew H. Morrison,
William L. Moore, J. J. Myres, H. H. Nettleton,
C. B. Nevin, F. H. Newcomb, Wm. A. Newcomb,
H. Hucks Newton, T. Franly Strowan, George H. Norton,
James O'Connor, Chas. E. Parker, Aaron Parker,
Michl. Parsons, A. S. Patton, J. E. Potter,
Francis C. Perry, Lemuel N. Peters, Joseph N. Philbrick,
Franklin P. Phillips, Lewis L. Pickard, John H. Ponce.

A SOUVENIR OF

INDEX.

ILLUSTRATIONS.

The State officers and the Executive Council are followed by the joint committees arranged alphabetically, while these groups are separated by miscellaneous pictures that have a direct or indirect relation to our State government, as follows: State House (page 4), Governor's Private Room, (6), Council Chamber (8), Senate Chamber (10-11), Room of President of the Senate (12), Senate Reception Room (14), Senate Reading Room (15), Room of the Speaker of the House (16), Doric Hall (19), The State Library (20), Hall of the House (96), House Reading Room and Writing Room (97), View from Cupola (98), House Corridor (100), Main Corridor (101), "Tom", Meagher the "candy man" (102), East Front of Capitol (103), The Old State House (104).

EXECUTIVE DEPARTMENT.

	PORTRAIT.	SKETCH.		PORTRAIT.	SKETCH.
Wolcott, Roger	5	105	Swallow, G. N.	9	109
Crane, W. M.	7	105	Sullivan, J. H.	9	108
Olin, Wm. M.	7	106	Atherton, H. H.	9	109
Shaw, E. P.	7	106	Shaw, E. H.	9	109
Kimball, J. W.	7	106	Joslin, A. L.	9	110
Knowlton, H. M.	7	107	Plunkett, Wm. B.	9	110
Ryder N. F.	9	107	Perkins, J. M.	9	111
Lovell, B. S.	9	108	Hamlin, E. F.	9	111

THE SENATE.

	PORTRAIT.	SKETCH.		PORTRAIT.	SKETCH.
Bailey, C. O.	21-39-43-87	113	Hodgkins, W. H.	45-87-89	115
Barber, H. R.	21-55-69-91	121	Holden, J. B.	79-83-85	120
Bennett, J. C.	31-45-81	113	R. W. Irwin.	27-49-87	122
Black, W. R.	27-67-81	111	Leach, W. W.	29-51-71	114
Bouve, W. L.	63 71-75-91	118	Mahoney, W. B.	65-69-75	114
Brigham, W. H.	63-79-83	116	Moran, W.	47-51-73	112
Chamberlain, L. E.	25-39-47	118	Morse, W. A.	43-45-49	122
Cook, W. H.	55-69 91	121	Parsons, H.	23-31-41	115
Crane, E. B.	65-81-87-89	120	Putnam, G. E.	21-25-67-71	116
Dallinger, F. W.	27-29-61	115	Quirk, C. I.	49-37-39	119
Davis, W. W.	37-43-53-49	120	Roberts, E. W.	31-93-95	118
Fairbank, W. H.	39 41-73-93	121	Roe, A. S.	25-33-85	120
Farley, J. B.	39-77-95	122	Rourke, D. D.	41-57 61-67	118
Flint, J. H.	33-47-49	117	Shaw, D. B.	53-55	118
Flynn, J. J.	29 33-89	114	Smith, G. E., Pres.	13-83	111
Folsom, C. E.	25-57-75	119	Soule, R. A	23-79-85	112
Gallivan, J. A.	59-83-95	119	Towle, W. W	51-61-71	119
Gauss, J. D. H.	39-65-73	113	Whittlesey, W. A.	23-93-95	122
George, S. W.	37-77-95	114	Williams, F. H.	49-59-83	117
Harwood, A. L.	53-79-89	114	Woodward, C. F.	57-61-63	116

HOUSE OF REPRESENTATIVES.

	PORTRAIT.	SKETCH.		PORTRAIT.	SKETCH.
Adams, A. F.	21	163	Crocker, T. W.	21-77	154
Allen, R. M.	31	150	Crosby, A. R.	27-35	127
Allen, R. E.	81	164	Crosby, H. V.	35-53	163
Allen, S. A.	47	139	Crouch, C. S.	73	139
Ames, Butler	45-63	148	Cullinane, Richard	51-85	131
Andrews, R. F., Jr.	47	160	Curtis, William	23	151
Anthony, J. C.	87	126	Dalton, J. F.	47	134
Apsey, A S.	39-71	142	Davis, D. W.	65 67	130
Attwill, H. C.	49	133	Davis, W. R.	87	141
Bachelder, T. C.	47-71	160	Dean, C. A.	89	149
Balcom, George	31	146	Dean, C. L.	95	143
Baldwin, J. E.	53-69	158	Denham, T. M.	37-69	128
Barnard, F. W.	31-51	127	Donahue, Thomas	51-69	129
Bartlett, G. H.	35-93	130	Donovan, E. E.	37	127
Bartlett, J. B. L.	35-89	161	Dooling, T. J.	37	138
Bates, J. L., (Speaker)	17	124	Drake, F P.	41	150
Battles, D. W.	59	155	Draper, H. J.	29	148
Beede, C. O	61	132	Driscoll, D. J.,	51	138
Belcher, H. A.	59	151	Dubuque, H. A.	49	129
Bemis, G. E.	21	136	Dumond, J. B	35-55	158
Bennett, F. P.	21-37	133	England, Daniel	79	126
Bickford, S. F.	61	162	Estes, E. B.	41-55	154
Bisbee, Horatio	21	139	Estey, F. W.	25	161
Blaney, O. C.	37	159	Farmer, F. H.	29	149
Bleiler, John	55	160	Farrar, F. F.	41 95	166
Bosworth, H. H.	29-89	138	Favor, John	93	135
Bottomly, Jerome	31	163	Fay, Asa B.	43	165
Boutwell, H. L.	47-57	143	Feneno, J. J.	55	159
Boynton, Warren	35-67	136	Fitzgerald, W. T. A.	61	156
Breath, M. L.	39-77	161	Folsom, A. T.	25	138
Bresnahan, H. W.	37	158	Foster, H. C.	81	135
Bridgeo, William	41	133	Francis, F. W.	45	128
Brooks, O. T.	89	162	Frederick, G. G.	57	131
Brown, C. E.	47	145	Fuller, G. F.	67-79	137
Bullock, W. J.	75	128	Gaddis, M. E.	53 77	159
Burgess, A. H.	25	165	Garrity, R. W.	51	159
Callender, E. B.	73-87	161	Gartland, J. J. Jr.	67	157
Campbell, Andrew	63	139	Gaylord, H. E.	81	140
Carberry, J. F.	77	167	Gilman, M. D.	25	166
Carleton, G. H.	95	130	Gleason, D. J.	43	158
Chandler, L. B.	73	142	Gove, Otis M.	23-79	145
Chapple, W. D.	71	134	Grant, O. S.	57	159
Clancy, J. B.	87	158	Grimes, J. W.	27 81	149
Clarke, Albert	83-95	152	Hall, Almon E.	55-95	125
Clerke, C. S.	61	157	Hall, Amos E.	23-91	143
Codman, J. M., Jr.	89	150	Hall, Luther	35 45	125
Cole, Samuel	25-39	135	Hammond, Fred	25	161
Conneily, J. W.	55	129	Harlow, F. P.	63	153
Conroy, T. A.	41	159	Harwood, G. F.	25	133
Cooke, W. S V.	87-91	164	Haskins, L. M.	79	135
Coolidge, D. S.	73	141	Hawes, M. E.	57	151
Coombs, G. W.	52-77	167	Hayes, A. S.	61	158
Crawford, F. E.	39-51	145	Hayes, W. H. I.	25-83	147

INDEX

	PORTRAIT	SKETCH		PORTRAIT	SKETCH
Hayward, A. F.	93	145	Myers, J. J.	49-83	140
Hemphill, A. E.	55-59	139	Nettleton, W. A.	27-33	126
Hill, J. W.	33-65	139	Nevin, E. B.	79	151
Hiscox, A. F.	21	164	Newcomb, T. H.	55	151
Hoag, C. E.	45	138	Newcomb, W. N.	69	140
Holton, S. A.	89	124	Newton, H. H.	49	143
Horgan, F. J.	71	157	Noonan, T. F.	49	155
How, C. F.	23	130	Norton, G. H.	33	159
Howard, W. F.	93	165	O'Connor, James	81	155
Howe, Rufus	65-91	147	Parker, C. E.	21	163
Hoyt, E. H.	87	131	Parker, Harold	87	165
Huntress, F. E	57	142	Parsons, H. C.	83-95	136
Innes, C. H.	49	157	Paton, A. S.	95	166
Johnson, C. R.	71	167	Pattee, J. E.	69	148
Jones, G. R.	61-83	149	Perry, F. C.	47-85	146
Jones, M. D.	29-85	142	Peters, L. W.	49	161
Jones, M. B.	29	129	Philbrick, J. M.	41-93	128
Josselyn, W. A.	87	152	Phillips, F. F.	33 77	142
Joubert, J. H.	39-53	131	Pickard, E. L.	61	145
Kane, D. J.	25	156	Ponce, J. H.	79	141
Keith, C. P.	61	141	Poor, Albert	79	131
Kells, William, Jr.	75-85	159	Porter, B. Jr.	33-91	127
Kelly, J. L.	59	155	Powers, J. A.	31	144
Kenefick, T. W.	83-95	137	Pratt, D. G.	67-93	153
Kiley, D. J.	47	157	Ramsay, J. P.	77-85	148
King, A. D.	21	137	Ramsdell, C. H.	65-77	133
King, R. V.	71	160	Reed, S. D	79	127
Kyle, W. S.	59	152	Rice, G. M.	63-93	166
Lang, W. A.	43-81	148	Richardson, F. S.	63-89	125
Learoyd, A. P.	53-85	132	Ross, L. W.	45	161
Leland, Francis	33	162	Ross, S.	51-53	128
Lewis, C. D.	23	146	Rowan, J. A.	55	156
Libby, J. F.	71	144	Rowell, E. T.	57-87	148
Lockhart, Alex.	87	129	Russell, M. L.	73	167
Lowell, F. C.	83	157	Saunders, C. R.	27-37	158
Lyon, A. W.	27 45	159	Sears, T. D.	43	125
Macken, L. J.	29	126	Seavey, J. F.	87	132
Mackey, Thomas	35-67	136	Selfridge, G. S.	27	171
Magenis, J. E.	49	125	Severance, W. H.	31	133
Mahoney, D. A.	35-75	157	Sheehan, J. F.	25	138
Mahoney, W. E.	27	155	Sisson, R. S.	73	132
Marden, W. H.	29-63	149	Skillings, W. E.	57-85	160
Mayo, B W.	63-81	137	Slocum, J. O.	41-43	128
McCarthy, J. J.	79 83	156	Smart, G. B.	31-75	131
McKnight, L. G.	23-63	163	Smith, H. C.	43-67	135
McLoughlin, W. J.	27-71	167	Snow, A. R.	69	164
McManus, J. A.	45	159	Stalker, H. L.	23-79	155
Mead, G. F.	61	144	Stanley, B. F.	81	130
Meek, T. H.	91	164	Staples, N. G.	35-53	153
Mellen, G. W.	91	126	Stebbins, M. M.	91	137
Miller, W. J.	49	156	Stevenson, J. M	43-73	126
Mills, C. P.	43-65	136	Stewart, J. I.	61	160
Montgomery, J. A.	93	141	Stone, W. B.	49-83	138
Morrison, A. H.	45	129	Sullivan, C. F.	23	131
Morse, W. L.	33	146	Swift, W. S.	41-65	129

	PORTRAIT	SKETCH		PORTRAIT	SKETCH
Taft, A. R.	91	164	Whidden, G. W.	85-89	145
Tague, P. F.	25	155	Whipple, J. J.	73-75	154
Talbot, Zephaniah	89	146	Whitaker, E. J.	49	152
Thompson, James	95	151	Whitcomb, F. H.	75	147
Tilton, C. W.	69	134	Whitcomb, G. L.	65-89	147
Trow, C. E.	79	134	White, H. C.	61	142
Tuttle, S. A.	57	150	Whitehead, James	51	129
Twomey, E. J.	31	156	Willard, E. E.	59	162
Waite, J. G.	95	143	Williams, A. P.	33	165
Washburn, C. G.	89	167	Williams, G. F.	93	152
Waterman, E. C.	73-75	153	Winslow, F. O.	59-65	150
Wells, A. E.	37-67	132	Wood, A. S.	39-69	149
Wentworth, E. E.	29	153			

ELECTIVE AND APPOINTIVE OFFICERS.

Bridgman, F. E.	17	168	Sanger, W. H.	13	124
Coolidge, H. D.	13	124	Taylor, K. T.	13	124
Dowse, Rev. Edmund	13	123	Waldron, Rev. D. W.	17	168
Kimball, J. W.	17	168			

SERGEANT AT-ARMS AND APPOINTEES.

Adams, J. G. B.	99	168	Mitchell, L. G.	99	171
Backman, E. S	99	171	Morgan, H. W.	99	171
Beatty, J.	99	169	Phillips, L. A.	99	170
Bean, A. G.	99	170	Philbrick, C. W.	99	169
Davis, C, G.	99	168	Pope, E. T.	99	169
Fillebrown, C. W.	99	171	Remington, D. T.	99	169
Gould, E. C.	99	170	Smith, C. J.	99	171
Holmes, S.	99	170	Sykes, H. W.	99	170
Ireland, F. A.	99	170	Tarbell, C J.	99	170
Kinnear, J	99	169	Taylor, R. J.	99	170
Legg, C. A.	99	169	Tucker, T. J.	99	169
Locke, J. H	99	170			

www.ingramcontent.com/pod-product-compliance
Lightning Source LLC
Chambersburg PA
CBHW031442160426
43195CB00010BB/823